WIRE MILL

This dam is full of fish! During the s
months maggot or sweetcorn will c
day long. Great for beginners with p
roach. perch, tench and a good head o
crucian carp. There are also a few large carp,
well into double figures.The high quality
roach and
perch also
makes this
water one of
the best winter
fishing venues
in the area.

WIRE MILL DAM
FISHERY

Whiteley Wood Lane
Ringinglow Road
Knowle Lane
Bents Road
Ecclesall Road

Fish-it2
South Yorkshire

Published by:
Arc Publishing and Print
166 Knowle Lane
Sheffield S11 9SJ
Produced By: Chris Keeling

Whilst every effort has been made to ensure the contents of this
publication are accurate at the time of publishing,
Arc Publishing and Print and those involved in producing the content of
"Fish-it 2" cannot be held responsible for any errors, omissions or
changes in the details of this guide or for the consequences of any
reliance on the information provided in it. We have tried to ensure
accuracy in this guide but things do change and we would be grateful if
readers could advise us of any inaccuracies they have found.

ISBN: 978-1-906722-38-8

ACKNOWLEDGEMENTS

I would like to thank the following for their
help in producing this guide:
South Yorkshire Tourism for the use of their map.
Clive Nuttall secretary of Catcliffe, Treeton Anglers Alliance.
Doncaster & District Angling Association.
Denaby Miners Welfare A.C.
Ben Warren for front cover photo.
Danielle Mustarde for proof reading the book.
All fishery owners and angling clubs who have kindly
provided information and to those that gave permission
to use images from their websites.

May 2015

Arc Publishing and Print
166 Knowle Lane
Sheffield
S11 9SJ
Tel: 07809 172872

Welcome...

...to the fourth edition of Fish-it 2 South Yorkshire!
Like many other anglers my time on the bank is limited, but I like
to grab a few hours fishing whenever and wherever I can.
With this in mind, I have put together this latest edition where
I've included new venues in the area and have updated all the
best day ticket waters from the previous edition. Many of these I
have fished myself and caught well, however I have also included
others where I struggled but still managed to hook the odd fish.

I have included photographs, price details, directions and maps,
rules for each water and types of fish stocked. Brand new to this
edition and to help you out on your first visit to each venue, I have
given you a top tip and a choice of best baits to use. Don't forget
to record your best catch at the bottom of every venue page.

Fishing attracts so many people, perhaps it's the solitude in often
beautiful surroundings and of course, the eager anticipation of
catching a big one!
The bank side can be almost hypnotic and
the desire to catch just one more fish has
spoilt many a meal.
I hope you find this book useful and wish
you good luck, good fishing and remember -
"A bad day's fishing is still better than a good
day's work!"

Chris Keeling

Contents

About this Guide

To help you locate a fishery the venues have been arranged into alphabetical order and split into two sections, fisheries and rivers. Their approximate location has been indicated on a map on page 6.

Fisheries and Rivers

Each page contains details of a fishery with information on the following:

Description: A brief outline of what the fishery looks like plus details on features such as islands, depths and the best places to fish.

Directions: Usually from the nearest city or town, or from the closest motorway junction.

Ticket Price: All day ticket costs plus details on concessions.

Species: List of species present many with estimated weights.

Rules/Bans: The restrictions set by the fishery on types of baits, hooks etc.

Number of Lakes: The number of waters available to fish at the venue.

Number of Pegs: The total number of fishing spots at each venue.

Best Bait: An idea of the best bait to use.

Nearest Tackle Shop: Nearest place to buy tackle and bait to each venue.

Facilities: What is available at each location i.e. cafe.

Telephone: The number of either the owner, angling club secretary or match organiser.

Species / Symbols

Coarse fish most commonly found in the South Yorkshire area.

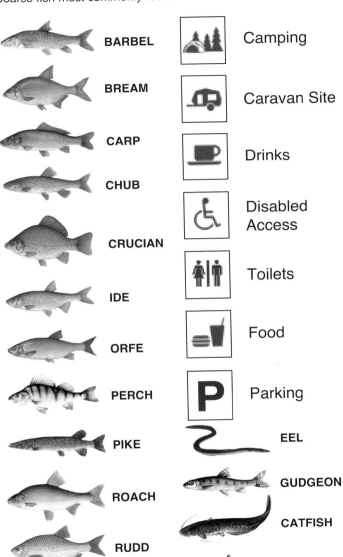

BARBEL

Camping

BREAM

Caravan Site

CARP

Drinks

CHUB

Disabled Access

CRUCIAN

Toilets

IDE

Food

ORFE

P Parking

PERCH

EEL

PIKE

GUDGEON

ROACH

CATFISH

RUDD

33 Location of fishery on the Map

TENCH

To help you find the nearest place to get tackle and bait, you will find a list of fishing tackle shops in South Yorkshire on page 78.

TROUT

5

Location of fisheries

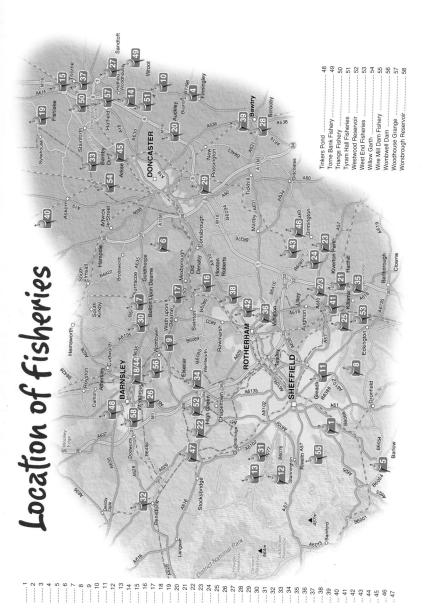

Abbeydale Dam
Abbeydale Road South, Sheffield.

Description: This well run water is between 4 and 5 acres in size. The depth varies from the dam wall end at around 20 feet to a foot deep at the far end. The 10 day ticket pegs which are next to the road are an ideal depth of between 5 and 6 feet. Fishing is very good from any of these pegs with the dominant species being rudd and tench. This is not a carp lake so don't expect to be snapped by a twenty pounder. The bank next to the railway line is for season permit holders only, contact the bailiff for details.

Directions: From the centre of Sheffield take the A621 (Abbeydale Road). After about 3 miles go straight on at the traffic lights at Beauchief. The Dam is 200 yards on your left just after the Hamlet entrance.

Top Tip
Try pole fishing at 6 metres for quality rudd on a single red maggot

Ticket Price: Day ticket £5.00 (£4.00 after 4pm)
Available from Woodseats Angling Shop.

Species: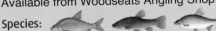

Rules/Bans: Barbless hooks, no groundbait, no meats, no boilies, no night fishing.

Facilities: Cafe nearby at the Industrial Hamlet.

Best Bait: Red maggot for the Rudd, Sweetcorn for Tench.

Number of Pegs: Ten

Number of Lakes: One

Nearest Tackle Shop: Woodseats Angling (see on page 78)

Telephone: 0114 2589578 or 0779 2657669

Best Catch	Peg No:	Weather:	Time of Day:	Date:
Species	Weight	Method (Line & Hook Size)	Ground Bait	Hook Bait

Aston Park Fisheries

Aston Ponds, Mansfield Rd, Aston, Sheffield.

SAT NAV S26 5PQ

Description: You are spoiled for choice with so many good pegs to chose from at this large seven pond fishery, but you can't go wrong fishing for carp with some luncheon meat on the Lily Pond. The waters have plenty of bankside features to target. Stable Pond is well worth a try as that too has plenty of large carp present. Lanta Pond is packed with fish but smaller and is more suited to the novice angler. This fishery has large stocks of silver fish. Bream and chub feature to 4lb with roach and perch to just over 2lb. There are some very big carp to over 30lb.

Directions: From junction 31 of the M1, take the A57 towards Sheffield, at the first roundabout turn left heading towards Killamarsh. Turn left after a few metres and follow the lane to the ponds.

Ticket Price: Day ticket £6.00. Concessions £5.00 (Dawn till Dusk) Night fishing is available by appointment only.

Species:

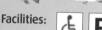

2
Fishery Location
See page 6

Facilities:

Best Bait: Meat for the carp. Pellet for the Bream

Number of Lakes: Seven **Number of Pegs:** 240

Nearest Tackle Shop: The Bait Bar tackle shop on-site. Next to the Waters Edge Cafe.

Telephone: Alex: 07743 845737
Shop: 07788 444452
www.astonparkfisheries.co.uk

Rules/Bans:

ASTON PARK FISHERIES
RULES

- BARBLESS HOOKS ONLY (MAXIMUM SIZE 12)
- NO BOLT RIGS OR FIXED FEEDERS
- 2 KEEP NETS TO BE USED FROM APRIL-NOV
- KEEP NETS ONLY TO BE USED IN MATCHES
- NO TINS ON BANK
- 2KG GROUNDBAIT (MAX)
- 1KG WORM, JOKER & BLOODWORM
- 1 TIN OF CAT MEAT (400g) PER DAY
- NO NUTS
- NO NIGHT FISHING
- NO FLOATING POLE IN MATCHES
- MAXIMUM POLE LENGTH 16 METRES
- GROUNDBAIT TO BE CUPPED IN OR THROUGH FEEDER
- 1 ROD PER DAY TICKET
- NO BRAIDED LINES
- ONLY ASTON PARK FISHERIES FEED PELLETS TO BE USED FOR FEED
- ALL EXCESS BAIT & LITTER TO BE REMOVED FROM SITE

THESE RULES ARE TO PROTECT THE FISH & FISHERIES

Best Catch	Peg No:	Weather:		Time of Day:	Date:
Species	Weight	Method (Line & Hook Size)		Ground Bait	Hook Bait

Aston Springs

SAT NAV S26 5PQ

Aston Ponds, Mansfield Rd, Aston, Sheffield.

Description: Ponds 1 and 2 formerly known previously as Laycocks Ponds are the first ponds you see. The three relatively new ponds are on your right and have been stocked with a variety of fish and are fishing well. Lake 2 has a good head of bream and some big carp to 27lb. The newly built platforms are excellent to fish from, plus the new cafe is very reasonable. Carp up to 27lb, bream, roach, ide, chub, rudd, and barbel.

Directions: From exit 31 of the M1, take the A57 towards Sheffield. At the roundabout turn left heading towards Killamarsh. Turn left after a few metres and follow the lane to the ponds.

Ticket Price: Day ticket £6.00. OAPs £4.00 Mon-Fri
Year permits £65.00 which includes KJS and West End Fisheries (13 ponds in total).

Species:

Rules/Bans: Barbless hooks only, keepnets in matches only. No ground bait except in pole cup or feeder.

Facilities:

Best Bait: Pellet or corn.

Number of Lakes: Five

Fishery Location
See page 6

Top Tip
Try copped worm or caster for the plentiful ide in the Snake Lake

Nearest Tackle Shop: Six am Tackle (See details on Page 78)

Telephone: 0114 2470876

Best Catch	Peg No:	Weather:		Time of Day:	Date:
Species	Weight	Method (Line & Hook Size)		Ground Bait	Hook Bait

McCallums Coarse Fishery

(Formally Bank End Fishery) Bank End Road, Finningley, Doncaster.

Description: McCallums has three lakes with the 34 peg match lake stocked mainly with carp. The other two lakes, of about 3 acres each, are open all year round. There's also an excellent shop which sells locally produced goods and has a cafe where you purchase day tickets. Most of the pegs are suitable for anglers with disabilities. I prefer West End Lake, as it's more sheltered. I did well fishing close to some reeds with a 5 metre pole, plenty of roach, perch, rudd and quite a few Chub present. The bream are now around 10lb. Loads of carp, the biggest is about 30lb.

Directions: Take the A614 to Blaxton. When you come to the crossroads with the Blue Bell pub, turn right onto the B1396. The waters are on the righthand side.

Ticket Price: Adults £6.00. Concessions £5.00

Species:

Facilities:

Rules/Bans: Under 16s MUST be accompanied by an adult. No dogs or radios. Carp over 4lb exempt from the keep nets (except for matches). In line method feeder only. No cat or dog meal allowed. Ground bait in pole or cup feeder only. Barbless hooks only. All nets must be dipped at Bank End.

Best Bait: I had a great day on sweetcorn.

Number of Pegs: 114

Number of Lakes: Three

Nearest Tackle Shop: Barrie's Fishing Tackle.

Telephone: 01302 770224

Fishery Location
See page 6

Top Tip

Fishing's great, but you must try the breakfast in the shop.

Best Catch	Peg No:	Weather:		Time of Day:	Date:
Species	Weight	Method (Line & Hook Size)		Ground Bait	Hook Bait

Barlow Fishery

Barlow Trout & Coarse Fishery, Barlow, near Sheffield.

SAT NAV S18 7TJ

Description: A great fishery for all ages and abilities. This well established fishery gives the angler plenty of choice with four coarse lakes and four trout lakes, plus a small brook. The four coarse lakes are stocked with a variety of fish with the largest carp being in the first two waters. The third pond is the tench pond and the last one is mixed. Plenty of good sized carp, rudd, bream, tench, roach, trout, barbel, and chub. The cafe serves a great bacon sandwich.

Directions: The fishery is located in the village of Barlow on the B6051, midway between Chesterfield and Owler Bar. Look out for the signs at the west end of the village.

Top Tip
Try fishing the margins, close to the reeds for the Grass Carp

Ticket Price: Coarse day ticket £5.00 After 1pm £4.00 Juniors, OAP's £4.00. Evening tickets £3.00. Matches by arrangement. Trout Lakes: Full day £20.00 three fish taken. £17.00 two fish taken. £15.00 catch and release.

Species:

Rules/Bans: No keepnets, no hard baits. Barbless hooks only.

Facilities: 🚻 🥤 🅿 ♿ 🏕 🚐

5
Fishery Location
See page 6

Best Bait: Maggots (whites and pinkies), sweetcorn, luncheon meat and in the summer, floating bread crust.

Number of Lakes: Four coarse, four trout.

Nearest Tackle Shop: Climax Fishing Tackle (see inside front cover)

Telephone: 0114 289 0543

Best Catch	Peg No:	Weather:		Time of Day:	Date:
Species	Weight	Method (Line & Hook Size)		Ground Bait	Hook Bait

Barnburgh Lakes

Ludwell Hill, Barnburgh, Doncaster.

Description: Barnburgh offers the angler a number of well stocked lakes accommodating both match and pleasure anglers.
The lakes are stocked with carp F1, bream, barbel, rudd, tench and roach. Depths are between 2 and 3 metres. If you can fish up to the island in Lake One, the fish seem to hold up there. Most pegs have been designed so that you can park behind them, this is ideal for the disabled angler.

Directions: From junction 37 A1(M) take the A635 towards Barnsley. Take your third left on to Blacksmiths Lane. Continue down this lane until you reach a T junction. Turn right onto Ludwell Hill, you will see the fishery about half a mile on your left.

Ticket Price: Day tickets £5.00. Concessions £4.00.

Species:

Facilities:

Rules/Bans: All Nets must be dipped on site. Barbless Hooks only max size 14. Barnburgh feed pellets only. No trout pellets, no cat or dog meat, no nuts. No floating poles or floating baits including bread. Ground bait only in cup or feeder. No litter to be left. No dogs, radios or wading. All under 16's must be accompanied by an adult.

Best Bait: Soft hookable pellets

Fishery Location
See page 6

Number of Pegs: 82

Number of Lakes: Three

Nearest Tackle Shop: Paul's Fishing Tackle Centre. or Tealys Tackle Shop (Details on page 78)

Telephone: 07752 528 086 or 07714 765 488

Top Tip
Take your fishing umbrella, there's little cover and it gets very windy.

Best Catch	Peg No:	Weather:		Time of Day:	Date:
Species	Weight	Method (Line & Hook Size)		Ground Bait	Hook Bait

Bolton Brickponds

Furlong Road, Goldthorpe, Bolton-upon-Dearne.

Top Tip
Recommend float fishing sweetcorn on the bottom for the tench.

Description: There are 3 inter-connected ponds to fish and with water around 28 feet in places, it's great for all year round fishing. There are plenty of different swims to fish and a lot of open grass areas for picnics. Most pegs are also accessible to disabled anglers. There are some huge carp in these waters, so make sure you take some heavy tackle if that's what you aim to catch. There are the occasional tench up to 8lb. Bream to 7lb, pike to 26lb, rudd, roach and crucian to 2lb. Carp well over 20lbs, plus a few chub.

Directions: Come out of Barnsley on the A635 heading towards Doncaster and turn off when you see a sign for Goldthorpe (B6098). Turn off right and follow the road through Goldthorpe and after a mile you will see the ponds on your left.

Ticket Price: Day tickets £3.00. Multi rods £6.00. Concessions £1.50, Multi £3.00. Year permits are available.

Species:

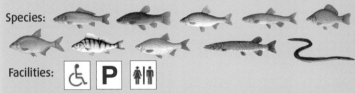

Facilities: ♿ 🅿 🚻

Rules/Bans: No keepnets, barbless hooks only. Permit required for night fishing.

Best Bait: Pop up boilies for the carp, sweetcorn for the tench.

Number of Lakes: Three

Nearest Tackle Shop: Tealys tackle Shop (see page 78)

Telephone: 07771 887800

Fishery Location
See page 6

Best Catch	Peg No:	Weather:		Time of Day:	Date:
Species	Weight	Method (Line & Hook Size)		Ground Bait	Hook Bait

Bradleys Ponds

Geer Lane, Ford, Sheffield

SAT NAV
S12 3YH

Top Tip
The local anglers use macaroni cheese, great if you can keep it on your hook!

Description: There are four ponds to try, I prefer the middle one which is also the largest at around two acres. This pond has a small island at one end which I fished up to using a 13 metre pole. I caught a few carp at an average weight of 8lb plus plenty of silver fish. This is a popular fishery so it is advised to arrive early to get a good peg, the fishing is also much better early on at Bradleys. There are also a few large catfish present in this lake, reported to be around 44lb! Set in an attractive valley of a working farm.

Directions: From the A6102 Sheffield ring road at Gleadless turn onto White Lane signposted Mosborough. After a mile turn right to Ridgeway. Follow the road till you reach Ford. Turn left after the pub on the corner and continue up Geer Lane until you reach the farm. The ponds are on your left.

Ticket Price: Day ticket £5.00. £3.00 after 4pm.

Species:

Facilities: P

Rules/Bans: No carp in keepnets, No cereal ground baits except bread punch, barbless hooks only. No dogs. No night fishing.

Best Bait: Macaroni cheese, banded pellet or meat.

Number of Pegs: Around 60

Number of Lakes: Four

Nearest Tackle Shop: Bankside Tackle (Details on Page 78)

Telephone: 01246 435563

8
Fishery Location
See page 6

Best Catch	Peg No:	Weather:		Time of Day:	Date:
Species	Weight	Method (Line & Hook Size)		Ground Bait	Hook Bait

Brampton Canal

(Elsecar Canal) Brampton Crescent, Brampton, Barnsley.

Description: Another stretch of disused canal that has been brought back to life for fishing. The water is an absolute picture with plenty of bankside vegetation giving some very interesting features to fish to. With plenty of pegs to choose from and parking near the bridge entrance, the canal is typical canal fishing. The water averages between 5 and 6 foot deep throughout its length with a maximum width of just short of 15 metres. Plenty of roach, ide, tench and the odd good bream and a few good carp.

Directions: Leave the M1 at Junction 36, get on the dual carriage way towards Wombwell. Go past Tescos to the roundabout, take your first left here and follow this road down for 100 yards and the water is accessible from the car park provided.

Ticket Price: Day tickets £4.00. Under 16s and over 65s £2.00. Year ticket £30.00. Concession £15.00.

Top Tip
Target two main areas of attack, one towards the far bank and one close in under the bankside vegetation.

Species:

Facilities: ♿ P

Rules/Bans: No bait bans only NUTS. No braided hooklengths. No double hooking. No floating baits. No tin cans allowed on bank. No carp in keepnets - except in matches. No floating baits.

Number of Pegs: Around 50

Best Bait: Corn fished over pellet on the far bank will take plenty of Tench. Maggot or caster during the summer months.

Nearest Tackle Shop: Fishing Republic (Details on page 78)

9
Fishery Location
See page 6

Telephone: 01226 203090

Best Catch	Peg No:	Weather:		Time of Day:	Date:
Species	Weight	Method (Line & Hook Size)		Ground Bait	Hook Bait

Candy Corner Fisheries

Wroot Road, Finningley, Doncaster.

SAT NAV DN9 3DZ

Top Tip
Bomb or method feeder towards the island on AJ's Lake – safe bet all year round.

Description: There are 4 lakes to fish at this venue. The largest water is known as AJ's and has 45 pegs with a depth of around six feet. Hoskers Lake which is smaller has 26 pegs and is also shallower, about five feet. It's stocked with a mixture of quality fish but the carp seem to be the dominant species. This fishery is very attractive and well kept, most pegs are suitable for disabled anglers.

Directions: From Doncaster take the A638 to Bawtry and follow the signs for Auckley. Turn left onto the B1396. Straight over at the roundabout in Auckley then take the first left signposted Wroot. After about a mile you come to the water on your left, just before a sharp bend.

Ticket Price: Day tickets £6.00 Concessions at £5.00
Fishing from 7.30 am till 7.30pm. Now open all year.

Species:

Facilities: Parking behind most pegs.

Fishery Location See page 6

Best Bait: 8mm feed pellet banded and loose fed - best all rounder for carp (pole, waggler, feeder)

Number of Pegs: 91

Number of Lakes: Four

Nearest Tackle Shop: Barrie's Fishing Tackle.

Telephone: 0776 9902731

Rules/Bans:

Candy Corner Fisheries Rules
1. Barbless hooks only
2. Maximum hook size 12
3. Keepnets only allowed in matches
4. No bloodworm or jokers
5. No boilies or trout pellets
6. The only pellets allowed are our own which can be purchased from bailiff on site (only one bag of each per visit)
7. No method feeder
8. No seed baits to be used
9. Ground bait in feeder or pole cups only
10. Maximum pole length 13 metres
11. No lime i.e. Corn or meat to be taken onto this fishery
12. No dogs
13. Under 16's must be accompanied by a adult at all times
14. All nets to be dipped
15. Do not discard unwanted bait into lake, it must be taken away
16. Anyone found fishing with barbed hooks will be asked to leave
17. Regular hook cheske will be carried out
18. Landing nets to be used at all times i.e. Landing and returning of fish
Thank you!
HAVE A GOOD DAYS FISHING

Best Catch	Peg No:	Weather:		Time of Day:	Date:
Species	Weight	Method (Line & Hook Size)		Ground Bait	Hook Bait

16

Carterhall Fishery

Carterhall Lane, Charnock Hall, Sheffield.

Top Tip
Try pole fishing the margins with soft hookable pellet or meat.

Description: The Top Pond consists of twenty concrete pegs placed along three sides of the pond, with two almost central islands reachable from most pegs. Luncheon meat hair-rigged with a small amount of ground bait in a feeder works very well between the islands. There are plenty of bankside features to target the many species in this pond. Bottom Pond which is still relatively new, has been stocked with 1000 ide and carp. Carp up to 23lb, bream to 3lb, tench to 4lb, perch to 2lb. Other species include roach, orfe, chub, rudd, and barbel.

Directions: Turn off the A6102, Sheffield ring road and head towards Ridgeway on the B6388. Take the third right turn into Carterhall Road. Turn left just after the school and follow the lane down to the farm. Look for the fishing sign.

Ticket Price: Day tickets £6.00 Concessions £5.00. All under 15's must be accompanied and supervised by an adult.

Species:

Facilities: ♿ 🅿 🚻   **Number of Lakes:** Two

Rules/Bans: No floating baits allowed. No cat or dog meat allowed. Max. 1kg dry ground bait - cup or feeder only. Barbless hooks only. No fixed feeders, ledgers or bolt rigs. No handling of fish with cloths or towels.

Best Bait: Luncheon meat or pellet.

Number of Pegs: Approx 40.

11 Fishery Location See page 6

Nearest Tackle Shop: Woodseats Angling (Details on page 78)

Telephone: 07803 877685

Best Catch	Peg No:	Weather:	Time of Day:	Date:
Species	Weight	Method (Line & Hook Size)	Ground Bait	Hook Bait

Cow Gap Farm Pond

Hill Top Road, Stannington, Sheffield.

Top Tip
Fish close to
the island with
sweetcorn to catch
the carp

Description: This small twenty peg pond has a huge variety of fish species for its size. The anglers who could reach the corners of the island in the middle were catching well using sweetcorn or pellet. I managed to catch plenty of rudd and ide close to the reed bed margins. Worth mentioning is that there is very little shelter at Cow Gap, but don't let that put you off, it's well worth a visit.

Directions: Head out of Sheffield on the B6077 Loxley Road. Take your next left after the Admiral Rodney public house. After 2 miles turn left into Lee Moor Lane. Follow to the T junction and turn right. After 300 yards turn left onto Hill Top Road. Follow the road until you see the fishery on your right.

Ticket Price: Day tickets £5.00. Concessions £4.00.

Species:

Rules/Bans: Barbless hooks only. No boilies. Groundbait in moderation. No cat or dog food. No keepnets except in matches.

Facilities: Cavavan and campsite near by.

Best Bait: Red maggot or sweetcorn.

Number of Pegs: 20

Number of Lakes: One

Nearest Tackle Shop: Dawson's of Hillsborough (Details page 78)

Telephone: 0114 2345234

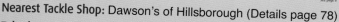

Best Catch	Peg No:	Weather:		Time of Day:	Date:
Species	Weight	Method (Line & Hook Size)		Ground Bait	Hook Bait

Damflask Reservoir

B6077 Loxley Road, Sheffield.

Description: Situated about 7 miles outside of Sheffield, Damflask covers 115 acres, so if you like your solitude while fishing this water is for you. There's a road that runs the full way around the reservoir making access from your car easy. The water has a wide variety of depths with about six feet at the inlet to almost 100 feet at the dam wall, but the majority of the water averages between 15 and 20 feet. Damflask is a renowned pike venue and gives excellent sport especially in the winter months. Bream averaging 2 to 3lb. Chub up to 6lb and perch to 4lb. A few tench and roach can be found. Pike run to around 34lb.

Directions: From Sheffield take the A57 towards Manchester. Then take the B6077 Loxley Road towards Bradfield, when you see the dam wall turn left.

Ticket Price: Adults £4.90. £3.60 for disabled, OAPs, and under 16s. Tickets purchased from a machine in the car park.

Species:

Rules/Bans: No keepnets, no ground bait, no night fishing, no live baits. Maximum of 4 rods for pike, and anglers targeting the species must be in possession of an unhooking mat.

Facilities: P

Best Bait: Luncheon Meat for the bream, perch can be tempted with a large lobworm.

Top Tip
Fishing mid-water, feeding hemp with caster on the hook can guarantee plenty of roach.

Fishery Location
See page 6
13

Number of Lakes: One

Nearest Tackle Shop: Dawson's of Hillsborough (see page 78)

Telephone: 07952 485798

Best Catch	Peg No:	Weather:		Time of Day:	Date:
Species	Weight	Method (Line & Hook Size)		Ground Bait	Hook Bait

Dale Pitt Lakes

Hatfield Woodhouse, Doncaster.

SAT DN7 6PH NAV

Description: Dale Pitt Lakes are former sand and gravel pits, which have been carefully and thoughtfully transformed into a superb fishing complex. Coarse and match fishing is on two separate lakes. Both Island Pond and the Stock Pond are approximately 3 acres with around 30 Pegs on each. The Specimen Carp Lake is approximately 7 acres with 15 exclusive, beautifully maintained and easily accessible pegs that allow room for all tackle and equipment including bivvies. It has been fully stocked with stunning common and mirror carp of up to 30lbs. Syndicate only on this water. The Trout Lake is around 7 acres with 30 custom-built and well maintained casting platforms. It is well stocked with both rainbow and brown trout.

Ticket Price: Day ticket (coarse) £6.00. Trout Lake. One fish ticket £15 (catch and release thereafter) Two fish ticket £20 (catch and release thereafter) Three fish ticket £25 (catch and release thereafter)

Species:    **Facilities:**

Rules/Bans: All nets must be dipped before fishing. Barbless hooks only (maximum size 10) No floating bait. No Meat. Keepnets for matches only. No dogs. Fishermen must sit at pegs (not from bank) All children under 16 must be accompanied by an adult. Only feed pellets purchased from Dale Pitt Lakes are to be used.
All excess bait & litter to be removed.

The following baits are permitted:
Any hook pellets allowed, sweetcorn, paste, hemp, worms, pinkies, squats, castors & maggots.

Directions:

Number of Pegs: 75

Number of Lakes: Four

14 Fishery Location See page 6

Nearest Tackle Shop:
Stainforth Angling Centre (details on page 78)

Telephone: 07500 865402

Best Catch	Peg No:	Weather:		Time of Day:	Date:
Species	Weight	Method (Line & Hook Size)		Ground Bait	Hook Bait

Delves Ponds

Selby Road, Thorne.

Description: A really good fishery to try with two lakes and plenty of features to target. Both lakes are stocked with most species and are of about the same depth - around 7 feet at the deepest. However I prefer the smaller of the two, fishing close to the island and catching every time. You'll find mostly roach and perch here but I had a couple of tench out. I think the larger lake does seem to be more for the carp angler. These ponds cater for both the novice angler and the more experienced pleasure fisherman. Ideal baits are maggot and caster for the roach and perch or meat for the carp.

Directions: From Junction 6 of the M18 head towards Thorne on the A614. Once you have passed the railway bridge look out for the fishery on the right.

Ticket Price: £3.50 a day. £2.50 concessions.

Species:

Rules/Bans: Keepnets in matches only, barbless hooks only.
No bloodworm or joker. No nuts or wasp grub.

Facilities:

Best Bait: Maggot, caster or meat.

Number of Pegs: Around 73

Number of Lakes: Two

Nearest Tackle Shop: Stainforth Angling Centre. (See page 78)

Telephone: 07920 103315

15
Fishery Location
See page 6

Top Tip
Try a maggot feeder to the centre of either pond for a good bag of roach

Best Catch	Peg No:	Weather:		Time of Day:	Date:
Species	Weight	Method (Line & Hook Size)		Ground Bait	Hook Bait

Elm Tree Farm Fisheries

Elm Tree Farm Court, Hooton Roberts, Rotherham.

Top Tip

Be careful pole fishing light in the margins, many large carp feed around the edges

Description: This venue consists of three lakes having recently been extended with the addition of a Strip Pond aimed mainly at the pleasure angler. The landscaping and pleasant surroundings make for a pleasurable day's angling. The carp lake is named Hooton Hollows, it's the smaller of the two older ponds with only 8 pegs. There is good depth throughout and will fish well at most times of the year. The lake is stocked with carp from 14lb to 27lb, it contains an island and has 42 pegs in total. Horseshoe Lake has a very good head of silver fish and carp up to 14lb. The on site facilities are very good with a cafe and toilets. Some pegs are suitable for anglers with disabilities and the venue has good access and parking.

Directions: Take the A630 from Conisbrough to Rotherham. When you reach Hooton Roberts take a right turn on to the B6090. You will see the lakes on your left.

Ticket Price: £5 Day ticket. £4 Concessions (OAP, disabled and children under 15 yrs) Carp Lake - £8 per person (2 rods) - over 18s only on this lake. If you are under 18 you may fish this lake if you are accompanied by an adult angler.

Species:

Facilities:

Rules/Bans: Barbless hooks only, no keepnets. All rules on-site.

Best Bait: Maggot, caster, corn, pellet, meat for the larger carp.

Number of Pegs: 58

Number of Lakes: Three

16
Fishery Location
See page 6

Nearest Tackle Shop: Parkgate Angling (Details on page 78)

Telephone: 01709 855219

Best Catch	Peg No:	Weather:		Time of Day:	Date:
Species	Weight	Method (Line & Hook Size)		Ground Bait	Hook Bait

Ferryboat Farm Fisheries

Ferryboat Lane, Old Denaby, Doncaster.

Description: This four acre lake offers a good selection of 69 pegs with plenty of room between them. There are now caravan and camping facilities on site, great for a long stay. The water depth is between 5-6 feet which is ideal for the many carp in here, some reaching 15lb in weight. Don't forget the reed margins as many good sized tench can be caught on sweetcorn or meat.

Directions: From the A1 Junction 36 take the A630 to Conisbrough. At the traffic lights turn right and head towards Mexborough on the A6023. When you reach a small roundabout, go straight over. Take the second turning on the left, signposted to Old Denaby. When you reach the village, turn right onto Ferryboat Lane, keep going till you reach the fishery.

Ticket Price: Day tickets £5.00, Under 18's must be accompanied by an Adult.

Species:

Rules/Bans: Barbless Hooks only.
No Keepnets. See notice board as you drive in.

Facilities:

Number of Pegs: 69   **Best Bait:** Sweetcorn or pellet.

Number of Lakes: One

Nearest Tackle Shop: Paul's Tackle Centre (Details on page 78)

Telephone: 01709 588088 or 07930 958605

17
Fishery Location
See page 6

Best Catch	Peg No:	Weather:		Time of Day:	Date:
Species	Weight	Method (Line & Hook Size)		Ground Bait	Hook Bait

Fleets Dam

Smithies Lane, Barnsley.

SAT S71 1NL NAV

Top Tip
Regulars all tend to fish off the bottom with either leger or a method feeder.

Description: The depth varies a lot on this water which favours the all year round angler. The bank closest to the car park is the shallowest at just over 4 feet. There is also a feature of a sunken wall about half way up the lake which can often be one of the better places to fish. This dam is around 10 acres and has 75 pegs to choose from. Carp to about 17lb, but roach and bream are the main species here. There's a few chub and plenty of tench present, plus the odd pike in the mid twenties. Parking is now available behind most pegs.

Directions: Take the A61 from Barnsley heading towards Wakefield. After about a mile take a left turn into Smithies Lane. Follow the road to the bottom of the hill and the dam is on the left hand side.

Ticket Price: Day Tickets £6.00. Concessions £5.00. Year Ticket £80.00 Concessions £60.00

Species:

Facilities: ♿ P

Rules/Bans: Barbless hooks only, no boilies or nuts.

Best Bait: Worm, paste, corn, meat and maggot.

Number of Pegs: 75

Number of Lakes: One

18
Fishery Location
See page 6

Nearest Tackle Shop: Barnsley Bait Company (Details on page 78)

Telephone: 01226 292579

Best Catch	Peg No:	Weather:		Time of Day:	Date:
Species	Weight	Method (Line & Hook Size)		Ground Bait	Hook Bait

Grange Farm Lake

Pinfold Lane, Fosterhouses, Doncaster.

Description: The owner has put a lot of fish in this lake, consisting mainly of pastie carp, with the odd much larger fish to over 11lbs. There are good stocks of tench that stick to the shelf and will take worm and corn freely. The small island and bankside features offer plenty of areas to target. This is a very popular well run fishery which can get busy so arrive as early as possible and check that there is not a match on. It's very well stocked with a variety of species making this lake ideal for the beginner to catch nets full of fish.

Directions: Leave the M18 at Junction 6, and head east towards Stainforth. Follow the signs for Fishlake, the farm is signposted from the road.

Top Tip
Try fishing close to the small island at the far end, this is a very good fish holding feature.

Ticket Price: Day tickets £6.00.

Species:

Rules/Bans: Barbless hooks only - no hook bigger than size 10. No cat or dog meat or biscuits, boilies, nuts or any trout pellets. Carp pellets are for sale on site. Keepnets and landing nets supplied by the fishery for pleasure or matches.

Facilities:

Best Bait: Maggot or caster.

Number of Pegs: 40   **Number of Lakes:** One

Nearest Tackle Shop: Stainforth Angling Centre (See page 78)

Telephone: 01302 846163

19 Fishery Location See page 6

Best Catch	Peg No:	Weather:		Time of Day:	Date:
Species	Weight	Method (Line & Hook Size)		Ground Bait	Hook Bait

Hayfield Lakes

Hayfield Lane, Auckley, Doncaster.

Top Tip
Don't ignore the margins. Many matches have been won with a bonus fish caught at your feet.

Description: Big Adams Lake offers 82 pegs and contains a wide variety of species but is best known for its large shoals of hungry brightly coloured carp. Dannie's Island Lake has 79 pegs and again contains a wide range of fish species, but is well known for the large ghost, common and mirror carp, which can be caught in huge numbers whilst fishing shallow in the summer months. Both Dannie's and Big Adams lakes also offer superb winter silverfish sport.

Directions: Leaving Doncaster on the A638 head towards Bawtry, cross over the M18 and then over the river. Continue until you turn left at the lights onto Hurst Lane. Follow Hurst Lane till you come to a second set of traffic lights. Turn left at these onto Hayfield Lane, follow the lane and you will arrive at the Lakes.

Ticket Price: Day tickets £6 for adults and £5 for concessions, extra rod tickets available at £2. An evening ticket is also available after 4:30pm at a cost of £4.

Species:

Rules/Bans: No keepnets (except matches) No night fishing. No barbed hooks. No hooks larger than size 10. Fishery's own feed pellets only.

Facilities: **Number of Pegs:** 161

(A good range of tackle and bait is available from the on-site tackle shop)

Best Bait: Meat or banded pellet.   **Number of Lakes:** Two

Nearest Tackle Shop: Barrie's Fishing Tackle (see page 78)
Telephone: 01302 864555

Fishery location
See page 6

Best Catch	Peg No:	Weather:		Time of Day:	Date:
Species	Weight	Method (Line & Hook Size)		Ground Bait	Hook Bait

Horseshoe Lake

 SAT S26 5RS NAV

Forge Road, Wales, Sheffield.

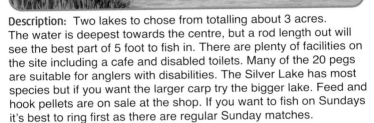

Description: Two lakes to chose from totalling about 3 acres. The water is deepest towards the centre, but a rod length out will see the best part of 5 foot to fish in. There are plenty of facilities on the site including a cafe and disabled toilets. Many of the 20 pegs are suitable for anglers with disabilities. The Silver Lake has most species but if you want the larger carp try the bigger lake. Feed and hook pellets are on sale at the shop. If you want to fish on Sundays it's best to ring first as there are regular Sunday matches.

Directions: Leave Sheffield on the A57 towards the M1, then turn onto the A618 signed for Killamarsh. Look for the sign for Wales and follow this into the village. Take a left turn into Manor Road, then 2nd right into Forge Road where the lake is situated.

Ticket Price: Day Tickets £5.00. (Tue-Sun) 7am till 9pm. Closed Mondays, except Bank Holiday Mondays.

Species: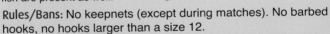

Several good sized gold fish are present as well.

Rules/Bans: No keepnets (except during matches). No barbed hooks, no hooks larger than a size 12.

Permitted Baits: maggots, pinkie, squats, caster, blood worm, joker, worm, carp pellets, carp pellet paste, All other baits and ground bait are banned.

Facilities:

Number of Pegs: 20 on the Big Pond, 12 on the Silver Pond.

Number of Lakes: Two

Best Bait: Carp pellets, worm or maggot.

Nearest Tackle Shop: Six A.M Tackle (see page 78)

21
Fishery Location
See page 6

Telephone: 01909 773826   **E-mail:** horseshoelake@talktalk.net

Best Catch	Peg No:	Weather:		Time of Day:	Date:
Species	Weight	Method (Line & Hook Size)		Ground Bait	Hook Bait

Howbrook Dam

Westwood New Road, High Green, Sheffield.

SAT
S35 4FD
NAV

Description: This dam is about 4 acres in size and has plenty of features to target. Depths vary from 4 feet at one end to over 18 feet at the dam wall. The wall is where plenty of tench and carp hold up. Big shoals of bream can be found with the largest fish at around 5lb. Good head of crucian carp with roach and rudd also present. Recently restocked with 1000 rudd, 200 tench and crucian. Take soft hookable pellets for the crucian carp and bream. This venue is not suitable for disabled anglers as access can be tricky.

Directions: Exit the M1 at Junction 36 and head towards Sheffield on the A61. After about a mile you will find the dam on the right. Parking is on the long lay-by.

Ticket Price: Day tickets £4. Permits £30, concessionary and over 65s permits £20. In the summer there are half price evening tickets (£2) from 5pm onwards.

Species: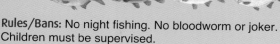

Rules/Bans: No night fishing. No bloodworm or joker. Children must be supervised.

Facilities: Parking and cafe in nearby lay by.

Best Bait: Maggot and pellet.

Number of Pegs: 40

Number of Lakes: One

22 Fishery location See page 6

Nearest Tackle Shop: Kerfoot's Fishing Tackle. (see on Page 78)

Telephone: 0777 3482033

> **Top Tip**
> Drip feeding a pint of maggots is the key to keeping the fish coming.

Best Catch	Peg No:	Weather:		Time of Day:	Date:
Species	Weight	Method (Line & Hook Size)		Ground Bait	Hook Bait

Kiveton Hall Farm

Kiveton Lane, Todwick, Sheffield.

Description: This complex offers very good facilities for both the match man and those interested in general coarse fishing. In all, there are three lakes on this complex with good car parking facilities adjacent to each one. In addition, there is also a café on site that serves good food at a reasonable price. The ponds have a mix of fish but the carp are what most anglers come here for, with the largest reaching around 30lb. Keep in mind, the water is very exposed and the sparsely planted trees do little to protect the water from the wind, so wrap up warm.

Directions: From the M1, Junction 31, head towards Worksop on the A57. At the first set of traffic lights, turn right on to Kiveton Lane and follow the road through Todwick, you will see the entrance to the farm on your left.

Ticket Price: Day tickets from £6.00. Under 16's £4.00. 3pm onwards £5.00. 5pm till dusk £4.00.

Species:

Rules/Bans: No bloodworm, joker, boilies, no ground bait. Keepnets only in matches. No night fishing. Barbless hooks are required and enforced.

Facilities:

Best Bait: Pellet or caster.

Number of Pegs: 86

Number of Lakes: Three

Top Tip
Fish up to the edges of the island in the Carp Lake this should guarantee a few fish.

23 Fishery Location
See page 6

Nearest Tackle Shop: D & P Fishing Tackle. (Details on page 78)

Telephone: 0114 2864179 or 07779 232505

Best Catch	Peg No:	Weather:		Time of Day:	Date:
Species	Weight	Method (Line & Hook Size)		Ground Bait	Hook Bait

Kiveton Waters

Hard Lane, Kiveton Park, Sheffield.

SAT NAV: S26 6RP

Top Tip
Try fishing a short pole down the margins, powerful elastic and 6lb line

Description: Kiveton Waters is a British Waterways fishery which has three lakes, total approximately 6.5 acres. One of them has been stocked with silver fish only. Most of the 81 pegs are suitable for disabled anglers. Try fishing Lake 3, which is the one with an island in the middle. This lake contains the larger carp running to the 15lb mark. They are as wide as they are long, a lovely looking fish that fight like mad.

Directions: From the M1, Junction 31, head towards Worksop on the A57. At the first set of traffic lights, turn right on to Kiveton Lane and follow the road to a T-junction. Turn left, then take an immediate right onto Hard Lane. After about half a mile you will see the lakes on your right.

Ticket Price: Day tickets £5.00. Concessions £4.00. Under 14's must be accompanied by an adult.

Species: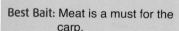

Facilities:

Best Bait: Meat is a must for the carp.

Number of Pegs: 81

Number of Lakes: Three

Telephone: 07789 954452

24
Fishery Location
See page 6

Nearest Tackle Shop: D & P Fishing Tackle. (Details on page 78)

Rules/Bans:

Fishery Rules

- Barbless hooks only, maximum size 12.
- Fishery nets only to be used.
- Ground bait in pole cups and feeders only.
- All feeders must be free running, no bolt rigs.
- No floating baits.
- Fishery feed pellets only to be used, maximum of 2 bags.
- No bait to be thrown in at the end of each session.
- No leaving litter.
- No tins allowed on pegs, all bait must be in bait tubs or bags.
- No washing cat meat in lakes must be done prior to arriving. (only 1 tin per session)
- No children under 14 years without adult supervision.
- Fishing 7am - dusk.

Best Catch	Peg No:	Weather:		Time of Day:	Date:
Species	Weight	Method (Line & Hook Size)		Ground Bait	Hook Bait

KJS Fisheries

Station Road, Killamarsh, Sheffield.

SAT NAV S21 1EN

Top Tip
Start fishing light to start with and only go heavier if the bigger fish move in.

Description: This well run fishery offers a great variety of sport. You could fish the first and largest pond as you drive in, this is packed with silver fish which can be caught on top during the summer months using bread or caster. The next lake you come to has more tench and crucian present. Next is the carp lake with fish up to 20lbs. There is also a small stretch of canal which has ideal pole fishing to the opposite bank.

Directions: From Sheffield head for Mosborough on the A6135. At the main junction in Mosborough turn left, signposted to Killamarsh. Turn right straight after going under a bridge on to Station Road. You will find the fishery at the end of the road.

Ticket Price: Day tickets are £6.00. OAPs £4.00 Mon-Fri. Year permits £65.00 which includes Aston Springs and West End fisheries (13 ponds in total).

Species:

Rules/Bans: No keepnets except on canal section. Barbless hooks only. See other rules on-site.

Facilities:

Best Bait: Maggot and caster. Soft hookable pellets for the crucian and bream.

Number of Lakes: 4 lakes, 1 stretch of canal.

Nearest Tackle Shop: Bankside Tackle (Details page 78)
Telephone: 0114 2470876

Fishery Location
See page 6

Best Catch	Peg No:	Weather:		Time of Day:	Date:
Species	Weight	Method (Line & Hook Size)		Ground Bait	Hook Bait

Lewden Spring Fishery

Station Road, Worsbrough Dale, Barnsley.

Top Tip

Ring and check there isn't a match on before you set off.

Description: A very attractive and well run fishery which is set in woodlands just outside Worsbrough. It has 40 pegs all with platforms. The best place to catch is close to one of the two large islands or tight to the many margin features. Meat, pellet or corn all work well for the carp. The depths vary from 7' 6" at the car park end down to 3' 6" in one of the pegs at the far end, but overall the depth is between 5 and 6 feet. Recently restocked with 600 1lb carp, 350 8-10" tench and 250 8-10" crucians.

Directions: From Junction 36 of the M1 take the A61 heading for Barnsley. When you reach Worsbrough turn right onto West street (A6100). After about a mile take your first right onto Station Road. Follow the road down the hill, when you reach a small bridge, the fishery is on your right.

Ticket Price: Day ticket £5.00. Under 16's £3.50.

Species: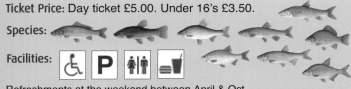

Facilities: ♿ 🅿 🚻 🍔

Refreshments at the weekend between April & Oct

Best Bait: Corn, meat or pellet.

Number of Pegs: 40

Number of Lakes: One

Nearest Tackle Shop: Barnsley Angling (see on page 78)

Telephone: Stuart on 07780 663822

Rules/Bans:

BAITS ALLOWED
MAGGOTS
CASTERS
WORM
CORN
CARP PELLETS
LUNCHEON MEAT

BARBLESS HOOKS ONLY
GROUND BAIT IN FEEDER
AND SMALL POLE CUP ONLY

NO BRAID - NO KEELNETS
ALL NETS MUST BE DIPPED

ALL CHILDREN UNDER 16
MUST BE ACCOMPANIED BY AN ADULT

26
Fishery Location
See page 6

Best Catch	Peg No:	Weather:		Time of Day:	Date:
Species	Weight	Method (Line & Hook Size)		Ground Bait	Hook Bait

Garbolino Lindholme Lakes

Don Farm, West Carr, Epworth, Doncaster.

SAT NAV DN9 1LF

Description: Lindholme Lakes is situated on over 100 acres of landscaped grounds boasting 8 lakes catering for all standards of fishing, from match to specimen to simple, lazy days on the bank fishing for pleasure. Willows and Laurels Lakes are very similar in size and shape and both have many species present. Beeches Lake is a pleasure and match lake with 40 pegs, superb fishing and a record catch weight of 298lb - has to be my favourite!
The Big Lake, which is over 150 years old, is where the bigger carp can be found.

Directions: From the M180, Junction 2 head for Belton. Turn right at the roundabout and follow the road to Sandtoft. When you reach the roundabout in Sandtoft take the second left and continue for nearly a mile. The fishery is signposted on your right.

Ticket Price: Day tickets are £6.50 with concessions at £5.50

Species:

Rules/Bans: No carp in keepnets, no dogs, no joker or bloodworm, barbless hooks only.

27 Fishery Location See page 6

Facilities:

Best Bait: Pellets, sweetcorn, meat & paste.

Number of Pegs: 505

Number of Lakes: Eight

Nearest Tackle Shop: On-site.

Telephone: 01427 872905

Top Tip

Try 4-6mm pellets or caster in summer months and maggot or worm in the colder winter months

Best Catch	Peg No:	Weather:		Time of Day:	Date:
Species	Weight	Method (Line & Hook Size)		Ground Bait	Hook Bait

Lodge Farm Fisheries
A638 Great North Road, Scooby Top, Doncaster.

SAT
DN10 6AX
NAV

Top Tip
Try fishing the
Top Pond for great
tench and
bream sport.

Description: Five great ponds at this venue with the top pond having mixed coarse fish with 46 pegs and depths of around 15 feet. The Lily Pond and Long Pond has mainly carp, chub, and bream with around 30 pegs each. Field Pond has 38 pegs with carp, bream, chub and barbel. Signal Lake has also got carp, bream, chub and a good head of tench.

Parking is at the rear of 90 per cent of the pegs with excellent access at the majority for disabled anglers. There's also an excellent cafe on site which is worth a visit.

Directions: Come out of Bawtry heading south on the A638. Lodge Farm is on the left just before Ranskill.

Ticket Price: Day Tickets £5.00. Concessions £4.00. Match £.00.

Species:

Facilities:

Rules/Bans: No keepnets (except matches),
All nets must be dipped on site, Barbless hooks max size 12, no in line or running method type feeders, no nuts, boilies, bloodworm or joker. All litter must be taken from site.

Number of Pegs: 185

Best Bait: Castor, maggot, pellet, worm and sweetcorn.

Number of Lakes: Five

Nearest Tackle Shop: R & R Sports (see on page 78)

Telephone: 0781 5030694

28
Fishery Location
See page 6

Best Catch	Peg No:	Weather:		Time of Day:	Date:
Species	Weight	Method (Line & Hook Size)		Ground Bait	Hook Bait

Loversall Lakes

Quarry Farm, Loversall, Doncaster.

Top Tip
Concentrate on the margins, it's easy fishing and the carp will find your bait at some point.

Description: There are two lakes of approximately 2 acres each which are well stocked with over 15,000 fish.
These include; mirror carp, common carp, crucian carp, ide, perch, tench, rudd, bream and F1s. The lakes have been beautifully landscaped and are now on their way to being well established.
"An angler fished a match on the bottom lake and then stayed after the match where he caught a carp of 18lb. 12oz. down the edge on luncheon meat. This is the biggest fish he'd caught and took ages to land." Well worth a visit.

Directions: Both the M18 and A1(M) motorways are near - it is close to the junction of the two motorways. The entrance is off the A60 between the superstore roundabout and Loversall village.

Ticket Price: £6 for adults and £5 for children/seniors

Species:

Facilities:

Rules/Bans: Barbless hooks only. No hooks larger than size 10. No bolt rigs. Loversall Lakes Fishery feed pellets only. No fish to be handled in towels or rags. Ground bait only through feeder or pole pot. No night fishing. No keep nets (other than in matches) No dogs. No litter / fires / hook lengths left on the bank. No boilies. No glass on the bank. No open cans on bank, e.g. sweetcorn, luncheon meat etc. No surface fishing.

Number of Lakes: Two   **Best Bait:** Luncheon Meat

29
Fishery Location
See page 6

Nearest Tackle Shop: Barries Fishing Tackle (see page 78)

Telephone: 07831189762 or 07860201906

Best Catch	Peg No:	Weather:		Time of Day:	Date:
Species	Weight	Method (Line & Hook Size)		Ground Bait	Hook Bait

Lowfield Lakes

Lowfield Road, off Station Road, Bolton Upon Dearne.

SAT
S63 8JF
NAV

Description: With three lakes to choose from at Lowfields there is plenty of room to fish. The top lake has around 30 pegs with a variation in depth from 7 feet on one side to 4 feet on the other. This lake holds medium to large size carp with a good head of bream and silvers. Corner Pond has 15 pegs and has some large ide, bream and carp. River Side Pond is the match lake which has 30 pegs and holds mainly carp and silver fish.

Directions: The lakes are on the Goldthorpe to Bolton road. When you reach Bolton Upon Dearne, turn left into Station Road. After the railway bridge the road joins with Lowfield Road. The fishery is on the right.

Top Tip
Powerful elastic is needed to control the many double figure carp present in all ponds

Ticket Price: Day tickets £6.00. Concessions £5.00. Season Ticket £100. Concessions £70.

Species:

Rules/Bans: Fishery Pellets only. No meat or meat based products. No Bloodworm or Joker. No Floating Baits. Groundbait in cup or feeder only. No surplus bait to be thrown in at the end of session. 2 nets required - Silvers / Carp. Max 75lb in one net Landing Net must be used. No fixed leads or fixed feeders. Barbless Hooks only.

Facilities:

Number of Pegs: 75
Some refreshments available.

30
Fishery Location
See page 6

Best Bait: Pellet in the summer, maggot in the colder months.

Nearest Tackle Shop: Tealys Tackle Shop (Details on page 78)

Telephone: 01709 888470   **Number of Lakes:** Three

Best Catch	Peg No:	Weather:		Time of Day:	Date:
Species	Weight	Method (Line & Hook Size)		Ground Bait	Hook Bait

Loxley Fisheries

Loxley Road, Loxley, Sheffield.

SAT NAV: S6 6SX

Description: Surrounded by mature trees and with numerous bank side features this is a very attractive lake. With only 32 pegs to choose from it can get busy on match days leaving only a few pegs for pleasure anglers. I like to fish close-in going for the barbel, that have now reached 7lbs. The place is absolutely solid with quality silvers and some big carp. The far bank is where the carp are being caught but if you like to catch barbel try the first few pegs on your left as you come in. This well run fishery has got to be worth a visit.

Directions: From M1 Junction 36, follow signs to Grenoside (A61) continue on to Hillsborough past Sheffield Wednesday's ground, turn right at Pizza Hut and go through Hillsborough centre on to Malin Bridge. Turn left at the Yew Tree pub; proceed along B6077 for 3 miles. Take the second left after the Admiral Rodney Pub.

Ticket Price: Adult £6.00. OAPs Mon-Fri £4.50. Under 16's £4.00

Species: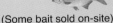

Facilities: ♿ P ☕ (Some bait sold on-site)

Rules/Bans: Barbless hooks only, no bloodworm, joker or boilies. Keepnets only in matches. No night fishing. See other rules on-site.

Best Bait: Meat or pellet.

Number of Lakes: One

Number of Pegs: 32

Telephone: 07711 429782 or 07860 372807

Nearest Tackle Shop: Dawsons Tackle Shop (see on page 78)

31 Fishery Location See page 6

Top Tip
If you want to catch barbel try and get on pegs 1-5, near the water inlet.

Best Catch	Peg No:	Weather:		Time of Day:	Date:
Species	Weight	Method (Line & Hook Size)		Ground Bait	Hook Bait

Nether Mill Coarse Fishery

Barnsley Road, Penistone.

SAT S36 8AD NAV

Top Tip

Try float feeder or small bomb, there's plenty of distance to cast to the islands.

Description: Nether Mill is a mixed fishery with the emphasis on carp and bream. This two acre lake has three islands and slopes quickly to around 6 feet. The 32 pegs are accessed by a path that runs all the way round making this very user-friendly for disabled anglers. There is a wide variety of species to interest every angler with common and mirror carp (to over 20lb), crucian and ghost carp, tench, bream (to 10lb), roach (to 3lb), rudd, chub, perch, brown trout and gudgeon.

Directions: Situated just off the Barnsley to Manchester road (A628). Turn off the A628 opposite the Nether Mill Coarse Fishery roadside sign, follow the signs through the farmyard and along a private road for 150 yards and park close to your chosen peg.

Ticket Price: Day tickets £5.00 available on the bank.

Species:

Rules/Bans: No keepnets, except during matches.
No night fishing, no dogs, no barbed hooks.
Also banned are nuts, cat meat and artificial baits.

32
Fishery Location
See page 6

Facilities: **Number of Pegs:** 32

Number of Lakes: One   **Telephone:** 07770 670042

Best Bait: You seem to catch most species on small sweetcorn.

Nearest Tackle Shop: Barnsley Angling (Details on page 78)

Best Catch	Peg No:	Weather:		Time of Day:	Date:
Species	Weight	Method (Line & Hook Size)		Ground Bait	Hook Bait

New Junction Canal

Barnby Dun to West End.

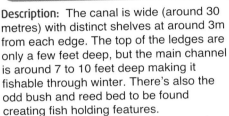

Description: The canal is wide (around 30 metres) with distinct shelves at around 3m from each edge. The top of the ledges are only a few feet deep, but the main channel is around 7 to 10 feet deep making it fishable through winter. There's also the odd bush and reed bed to be found creating fish holding features.

The main species found here are roach and perch to around 1lb, but eels, chub and bream can put in an appearance if you're in the right place at the right time.

The safest ploy is to fish the pole at the bottom of the ledge and as far out as you can manage in the weather conditions on the day. Pinkies, maggots, caster and worms are all safe bets.

Ticket Price: Day ticket £4.00. Books are valid from April 1st at £22.00. Concessionary rates £17.00 available for OAP's and Juniors.

Species:

Rules/Bans: Barbless hooks only. No vehicles on banks.

Facilities: None

Best Bait: Maggot and caster.

Number of Pegs: 557

Number of Lakes: One

Nearest Tackle Shop: Stainforth Angling Centre (see page 78)

Telephone: 07771 986849

> **Top Tip**
> Try ground bait for the bream and skimmers, or tight to the far bank for Chub

33
Fishery Location
See page 6

Information kindly supplied by Doncaster & District Angling Association.

Best Catch	Peg No:	Weather:		Time of Day:	Date:
Species	Weight	Method (Line & Hook Size)		Ground Bait	Hook Bait

Newbiggin Pond

A616, Lower Newbiggin, Tankersley.

Top Tip
Pole fishing soft hookable pellets produces good catches of crucian.

Description: A very attractive small pond with only 12 pegs - so arrive early to avoid disappointment. Two pegs are suitable for disabled anglers but it can be a bit noisy from traffic on the A616. The depth varies from 3 feet to 6 feet in the middle. The pond is well stocked with good size and quality fish with carp up to 15lb, bream up to 5lb, tench also up to 5lb, chub up to 4lb, crucians to about 2lb, ide between 3 & 4lb and a good selection of roach and perch to about 1.5lb. Most methods will catch you fish with maggot and pellet being the favoured baits with the regulars.

Directions: From Junction 36 of the M1 take the A61 heading for Sheffield. At the roundabout turn left onto the A616 heading back to the M1. After about a mile turn left into Park Lane and left again into the fishery car park.

Ticket Price: Day tickets £4.00
Permits £30. Concessions £25.

Species: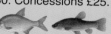

Rules/Bans: There are a few common sense rules; landing nets to be assembled before fishing commences, rods not to be left unattended, barbless hooks only, no keepnets and of course all rigs must be free running.

Facilities: **Best Bait:** Maggot and pellet

Number of Lakes: One   **Number of Pegs:** 12

Nearest Tackle Shop: Barnsley Angling (see page 78)
Telephone: 0779 9447145

34
Fishery Location
See page 6

Best Catch	Peg No:	Weather:		Time of Day:	Date:
Species	Weight	Method (Line & Hook Size)		Ground Bait	Hook Bait

Norwood Fishery

Cinder Lane, off Mansfield Road, Killamarsh, Sheffield.

SAT NAV S21 2AT

Top Tip
Fish the left side of the large pond, slightly shallower but more protection from the wind.

Description: This fishery is getting better with age and is already popular with match anglers. Try fishing close up to the islands in the larger pond. This is where I caught most of a dozen or so carp, all of which weighed around 6lbs. Depths vary from one end to the other, I prefer the shallower end near the stock pond. Fishing close to the reed beds also produces good weights. It's well worth a visit but pick a still day as there is very little shelter from the wind. Carp mainly in the 5-6lb bracket with a few reaching 15lbs. Bream to 8lb. Tench to 5lb. Plenty of roach, perch and ide.

Directions: From Junction 31 of the M1, head towards Sheffield. At the first roundabout take a left turn. Go past the entrance to Rother Valley. When you reach a small roundabout turn left and go up the hill. You will come across a small turning on your left about a 1/4 of a mile up the hill. Follow the track to the fishery.

Ticket Price: Day tickets £5.00 on the bank.

Species:

Facilities: P 🚻 🍴

35
Fishery Location
See page 6

Rules/Bans: Barbless hooks only. No floating baits. No keepnets except in matches.

Best Bait: Pellet is my choice bait here, but take along meat and corn as well. Maggot and caster for the roach and perch.

Number of Pegs: 34

Number of Lakes: Two

Nearest Tackle Shop: Bankside Tackle. (Details on page 78)

Telephone: 0114 2489224

Best Catch	Peg No:	Weather:		Time of Day:	Date:
Species	Weight	Method (Line & Hook Size)		Ground Bait	Hook Bait

Pinch Mill Fisheries

Pinch Mill Lane, Whiston, Rotherham.

Top Tip
Try fishing up to the central island, the larger carp seem to congregate around it.

Description: There are two lakes to fish and both are tree lined making this a very attractive venue. Both ponds are of a similar size. The first one you come to has 26 pegs and is between 6 and 8 feet deep. The other pond has 17 pegs and is shallower at around 4 foot. Most pegs are suitable for anglers with disabilities. There are plenty of ide that run to almost 3lbs, but most average just over the pound mark. There are a few carp present to 22lb, plenty of tench to 4lb, and barbell to 2lb. Good head of perch present.

Directions: Come off the M18 at Junction 1 and head towards Rotherham on the A631. At Worrygoose roundabout turn left and head for Thurcroft on the B6410. After a sharp left hand bend you will come across the fishery, around 200 yards on the left.

Ticket Price: £5.00 per day. £7.00 for 2 rods. Night Fishing: £15 for 24 hours.

Species:

Facilities:

Rules/Bans: No keepnets, barbless hooks only. No boilies, no trout pellets. Ground bait from pole cup or feeder only.

Best Bait: Sweetcorn or pellet and large chunk of meat for the carp.

Number of Pegs: Around 30

Number of Lakes: Two

Nearest Tackle Shop: Parkgate Angling Centre (Details Page 78)

Telephone: 07855 312963

Best Catch	Peg No:	Weather:		Time of Day:	Date:
Species	Weight	Method (Line & Hook Size)		Ground Bait	Hook Bait

Pine Lake fisheries

Oak Field Farm, Kirton Lane, Thorne.

Description: This venue has been established since 2006, since then it has been regarded as one of the most even match venues in the area. It's not because of the shape of the waters or even the depths, it's the breed of fish which has been stocked.

Ide are a very strong and powerful fish for their size, it's possible to catch great weights in short periods. The match record stands at 119lbs, not bad for 1lb fish on average.

Stock includes Carp, F1's, tench, ide, rudd and roach.

Directions: From the centre of Thorne take the A614. Cross the canal and turn right onto Kirton Lane. Follow the lane towards the M18. The fishery is on your left just before the motorway.

Ticket Price: Day Tickets are £5.00 which includes a landing net head. Keepnet Hire £1.00

Species:

Facilities: ♿ 🅿 🚻 🥤

Rules/Bans: No boilies, hemp, cat & dog meat, bloodworm, joker, tiger nuts, braided hook lengths, bolt rigs. You must use the landing net provided by the fishery.

Best Bait: Sweetcorn or pellet over a bed of micro pellets.

Number of Lakes: Two   Number of Pegs: 41

Nearest Tackle Shop: Thorne Pet & Angling (see page 78)

Telephone: 07867 553645

Best Catch	Peg No:	Weather:		Time of Day:	Date:
Species	Weight	Method (Line & Hook Size)		Ground Bait	Hook Bait

43

Ravenfield Ponds

Arbour Lane, Ravenfield, Rotherham

SAT S65 4ND NAV

Description: Ravenfield Ponds has six angling ponds set in a beautiful secluded valley which is rich in wildlife and was once part of the Ravenfield Park estate. Great Pond is the largest of the ponds at almost 3 acres, it's stocked with loads of skimmer bream, some going to 4lbs, tench to over 6lbs, perch to 4lbs, roach and crucian carp to 2lbs and plenty of rudd. Kingfisher Pond has a large proportion of crucians and tench together with some decent bream and huge perch. New Pond is small with approximately 15 pegs with a depth of around 5 feet, it's stuffed with skimmers, crucian carp, perch, roach, rudd and particularly tench. There is also a Specimen Lake solely for the use of carp anglers.

Directions: Come off the M18 at Junction 1. Head towards Bramley. In Bramley take the B6093 to Ravenfield. Just before you reach Ravenfield turn right on to Garden Lane. Follow this road which takes a sharp left turn and becomes Arbour Lane. Follow the lane to the ponds.

Ticket Price: Adult Membership £60. Joint Membership £100. Young Adult or Student £30. Under 16's £10.

Species:

Rules/Bans: All rules are available with your permit.

Facilities: 38 Fishery Location See page 6

Top Tip
Pole fish New Pond with soft hookable pellet over a bed of micro feed pellets

Best Bait: Maggots, casters, pellets and bread.

Number of Lakes: Six, plus stretch of S/Y Canal and River Don.

Nearest Tackle Shop: Parkgate Angling Centre. (See page 78)

Telephone: Phoenix & Parkgate Angling Club Tel: 01709 363788

Best Catch	Peg No:	Weather:		Time of Day:	Date:
Species	Weight	Method (Line & Hook Size)		Ground Bait	Hook Bait

Riverside Fishery

Gibbet Hill Lane, Bawtry, Doncaster.

SAT NAV DN10 6BT

Description: The lakes here have been completely restocked with a good variety of quality fish. Ricky's Lake has 45 pegs, Strip Lake has 10 pegs, and Sandmartin Lake has 20 pegs. They are all similarly stocked with carp to 18lb, crucian and ide to about 1lb and tench to 3lb. All the lakes have a depth of around 5 feet. The river next to the lakes can also be fished.

Directions: Take the A614 from Bawtry and head south towards the A1(M). Gibbet Hill Lane is on your left. You will see the entrance straight away on your right.

Top Tip
Try and find the ide by lightly feeding an area and pulling through looking for bites.

Ticket Price: £5.00 per day, £4.00 Concessions.
£6.00 Matches, £5.00 Match Concessions.

Species:

Rules/Bans: No keepnets except for matches, barbless hooks only.

Facilities: ♿ P 🚻 🥤   **Number of Pegs:** 75

Best Bait: Soft hookable pellet over a micro feed pellets.

Number of Lakes: Three

Nearest Tackle Shop: D & P Tackle (Details on Page 78)

Telephone: 01302 711889

Fishery Location
See page 6
39

Best Catch	Peg No:	Weather:		Time of Day:	Date:
Species	Weight	Method (Line & Hook Size)	Ground Bait	Hook Bait	

Roan Fisheries

Norton Common Road, Norton, Doncaster.

SAT DN6 9HP NAV

Top Tip
Keeping small amounts of feed going in does the trick!

Description: This 2.5 acre lake is spring fed by naturally occurring springs and has been stocked with a good head of F1 carp, crucian carp, bream, rudd, roach, chub, and barbel.
There are 43 pegs available all of which are 'all weather' wooden custom made swims. There is ample parking on-site and several areas of the lake have been designed with the disabled angler in mind - two of the swims have been built to facilitate the use of wheelchairs. The reed beds to either side of the pegs are excellent holding areas for most species.

Directions: From A1(motorway) Northbound. Take junction signposted Pontefract, take first turning right going over the A1 then your first left signposted Campsal. After about 500m turn left signposted Norton after about 2km turn right at the junction signposted Norton. Go all the way through Norton Village, cross over the railway line and the fishery is about 200m on the left.

Ticket Price: Adult: 1 Rod - £5.00. 2 Rods - £8.00.
Concessionary: 1 Rod - £4.00. 2 Rods - £6.00

Species:

Facilities: **No of Pegs:** 43
Number of Lakes: One

Rules/Bans: Barbless hooks only - maximum hook size 12. No keep nets except during matches. All nets must be dipped in the solution provided. No Method Feeders. No braided line. Rods and equipment must not be left unattended. No radios to be played when fishing. No Dogs allowed around the fishery at any time. No children under 14 to be left unsupervised. Only fishery nets to be used. **Bait Rules:** No Floating Baits (inc Bread and Pellets) No Trout Pellets, Boilies, Peanuts, Tigernuts, Bloodworm and Joker. Only Coarse pellets purchased from Roan Fishery may be used as a feed bait.

Best Bait: Meat or pellet.

Nearest Tackle Shop: The on-site tackle shop has a good range of bait and tackle from hooks to poles, pellets to maggots.

Telephone: 01709 552965   **Mobile:** 07891 593870

40
Fishery Location
See page 6

Best Catch	Peg No:	Weather:		Time of Day:	Date:
Species	Weight	Method (Line & Hook Size)		Ground Bait	Hook Bait

Rother Valley Country Park

Mansfield Road, Wales Bar, Sheffield.

SAT NAV S26 5PQ

Description: There are three places to choose from, Northern Lake, Nethermoor Lake and a long stretch of the River Rother. The two lakes contain plenty of perch, roach and carp, but many anglers prefer to fish the river where there has been some large chub caught. The river bank can be overgrown with nettles so be prepared to hack a space for yourself, but trust me it will be worth it! The lakes can be busy with other sports going on so leave the lakes and try the river at the weekends.

Directions: From the M1 Motorway Junction 31, follow signs to Sheffield city centre. At the first roundabout turn left onto the A618. Rother Valley is on the right after 2 miles.

Top Tip
Try trotting on the river with a single red maggot for the chub

Ticket Price: Day Ticket £4.70 for up to 2 rods.
Day Ticket concessionary price £3.70 over 60 years and under 16 years. Day tickets can be purchased from the parking barrier or at the bank side from park staff.

Species:

Facilities: ♿ P 🚻 🍴 **Number of Pegs:** N/A

Rules/Bans: No cereal ground bait. Barbless hooks only.

Best Bait: Maggot on the river, pellet on the lakes.

41
Fishery Location
See page 6

Number of Lakes: Two, plus a stretch of the River Rother.

Nearest Tackle Shop: Bankside Tackle (Details on page 78)

Telephone: 0114 2471452

Best Catch	Peg No:	Weather:		Time of Day:	Date:
Species	Weight	Method (Line & Hook Size)		Ground Bait	Hook Bait

Roundwood Ponds

SAT S62 6BU NAV

Aldwarke Lane, Rotherham.

Description: Two ponds to chose from; one large pond with around 40 pegs. This larger pond boasts very good carp up to 33lb with plenty of quality tench. The best place to fish is in the nearest corner of the largest pond. Bring some heavy tackle as these carp put up a good fight. The smaller lake has about 20 pegs and is a pole and waggler only water. It has lots of smaller carp to mid-doubles along with tench to 4lb, roach, perch and skimmers.

Directions: From the centre of Rotherham head towards Doncaster on Fitzwilliam Road. When you reach a large round about called the Mushroom roundabout, take your first left on to Aldwarke Lane. Continue to the last entrance of the steel works and follow the track down to the ponds.

Ticket Price: Day Ticket £5.00. Concession £4.00
2 Rods £6.50. Night Ticket £15.00. 24Hr Ticket £20.00

Species:

Rules/Bans: Barbless hooks only, no boilies, no tiger nuts, no braided line, up to size 12 hooks only.

Facilities: P   **Best Bait:** Bread, Sweetcorn and prawn.

Number of Pegs: Around 60

Number of Lakes: Two

Telephone: 0114 2873070

Nearest Tackle Shop: Six Am Tackle and Bait (Details on Page 78)

42 Fishery Location See page 6

Top Tip

Try bread, fished at half-depth or pop-up Sweetcorn

Best Catch	Peg No:	Weather:		Time of Day:	Date:
Species	Weight	Method (Line & Hook Size)		Ground Bait	Hook Bait

Side farm fishery

Laughton Common Road, Thurcroft, Rotherham.

Top Tip
Try small bits of luncheon meat down the margins or close to the island

Description: This relatively new fishery has become very popular with pleasure anglers. This is a busy match venue so check before hand that there is space to fish. Their are 39 pegs which all have reeds to the side of them, many carp can be seen moving them while feeding. Depth varies between 3 and 6 feet. Try fishing up to the island that runs the full length of the pond. This can only be reached with a long pole or ideally a feeder rod using sweetcorn on the hook. This is a great venue but it has little protection from the wind.

Directions: From the M1, Junction 32 take the M18. Exit at Junction 1 and turn right heading for Hellaby. As soon as you leave the roundabout turn right. Continue down this road until you reach a T junction at Thurcroft. Turn left onto the B6060 and follow this road through Thurcroft. After a mile the road bends sharply left, after 200 yards you will see the fishery sign on your left.

Ticket Price: £5.00 per day. Concessions £4.00

Species:

Facilities:

43 Fishery Location See page 6

Best Bait: Pellet, sweetcorn or meat.

Number of Pegs: 39

Number of Lakes: One

Nearest Tackle Shop: Wickersley Angling Centre (Details on page 78)

Telephone: 07909 758724

Rules/Bans:

SIDE FARM FISHERY
Tel 07909 758724
FISHERY RULES

1 PERMITTED BAITS
  MAGGOTS
  CASTORS
  CARP PELLETS ONLY (UP TO 6 mm)
  SWEETCORN
  LUNCHEON MEAT (UP TO 1 TIN)
2 GROUNDBAIT IN A FEEDER OR POLE CUP
  UP TO 1 KG
3 BARBLESS HOOKS ONLY (NO MICRO BARBS)
4 MAX HOOK SIZE 12
5 NO KEEPNETS EXCEPT FOR MATCHES
6 ALL NETS ARE PROVIDED BY THE FISHERY
  NO OTHERS ARE ALLOWED
7 PLEASE USE THE LITTER BINS PROVIDED
8 NO DOGS ALLOWED
9 NO CHILDREN UNDER THE AGE OF 15
  UNLESS SUPERVISED BY AN ADULT
ANYONE FOUND BREAKING THESE RULES
WILL BE BANNED

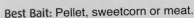

Best Catch	Peg No:	Weather:		Time of Day:	Date:
Species	Weight	Method (Line & Hook Size)		Ground Bait	Hook Bait

Smithies Reservoir
Smithies Lane, Barnsley.

SAT
S71 1NL
NAV

Top Tip

If meat fails, try fishing paste just touching the bottom

Description: The reservoir has recently been stocked with a ton in weight of F1 carp, anglers are reporting 100lb bags in the warmer months on all methods. Barnsley & District Amalgamated Angling Society also stocked the pond with more carp around the 2-4lb mark, so if it's carp your after this is the place to fish. There are matchers held mid week and weekends in the warmer months, so it's best to check the notice board in the car park to save disappointment. Good condition pegs make it suitable for disabled anglers.

Directions: From Barnsley head towards Wakefield on the A61. After only half a mile from Barnsley town centre take a left turn into Smithies Lane. Follow the road to the bottom and you will see the water on your righthand side.

Ticket Price: Day tickets £4.00. Under 16s and over 65s £2.00. Year ticket £30.00. Concession £15.00.

Species:

Rules/Bans: No bait bans only nuts. No braided hooklengths. No double hooking. No floating baits. No tin cans allowed on the bank. No carp in keepnets - except in matches.

Facilities: **Number of Lakes:** One

Best Bait: The carp catch well on meat as do the tench. Caster and maggot are ideal for the roach and perch.

Fishery Location
See page 6

Nearest Tackle Shop: Barnsley Bait Company (Details page 78)

Telephone: 01226 203090

Best Catch	Peg No:	Weather:		Time of Day:	Date:
Species	Weight	Method (Line & Hook Size)		Ground Bait	Hook Bait

South Yorkshire Navigation Canal

Doncaster to Long Sandall.

You can park right behind your peg at Long Sandall

Barnby Dun Swing Bridge

The Canal near Barnby Dun. Thorpe Marsh Power Station in the background.

Description: The canal runs parallel to the River Don where the river isn't navigable. The canal water runs from above the Prison at Doncaster, through Doncaster, Wheatley, Long Sandall, Kirk Sandall, and Barnby Dun before it splits to form the New Junction Canal and Stainforth & Keadby Canal at Bramwith. The width is around 25 metres and depth is around 8 feet down the track. Roach, skimmers, hybrids, perch and gudgeon are the most common fish, but chub and bream can show occasionally. On still days when the tow on the canal is almost still, a waggler can be very productive.

Ticket Price: Day ticket £4.00. Books are valid from April 1st at £22.00. Concessionary rates £17.00 available for OAP's and Juniors.

Species:

45
Fishery Location
See page 6

Rules/Bans: Barbless hooks only. No vehicles on banks.

Facilities: None

Best Bait: Maggot or pinkie.

Number of Lakes: One

Nearest Tackle Shop: Stainforth Angling Centre

Telephone: 07771 986849

Top Tip

Try a ground bait feeder or bomb, tight to a far bank feature for the chub

Information kindly supplied by Doncaster & District Angling Association.

Best Catch	Peg No:	Weather:		Time of Day:	Date:
Species	Weight	Method (Line & Hook Size)		Ground Bait	Hook Bait

Straight Mile Fishery

Common Road, Brampton, near Dinnington

Description: The lake is made up of four strips separated by three islands, with plenty of features to target. You will catch in the middle, near the islands or close in. This is a year - round fishery with 100lb nets recorded. This is one of the largest match angling fisheries in the area, boasting 90 pegs. The venues prolific roach stocks mean that bites are rarely hard to come by. It's virtually guaranteed while fishing light for roach and rudd that a good sized carp or barbel will take your bait making a real mess of your rig.

Directions: From the M1 Motorway Junction 31 take the A57 to Worksop. Turn left at the first set of traffic lights. After about half a mile turn left again into Pocket Handkerchief Lane. At the end of the lane turn left and the fishery is on your left hand side.

Ticket Price: Day ticket £5.00

Species:

Rules/Bans: Barbless hooks only.
Juniors Must be accompanied by an adult.

Top Tip
Using a margin pole, you can often pick up fish right under your feet.

Facilities:

Best Bait: Luncheon meat, corn, maggot and caster are the only baits allowed on the fishery.

Number of Pegs: 90   **Number of Lakes:** One

Nearest Tackle Shop: D & P Tackle (Details on page 78)

Telephone: 07771 9953310

46
Fishery Location
See page 6

Best Catch	Peg No:	Weather:		Time of Day:	Date:
Species	Weight	Method (Line & Hook Size)		Ground Bait	Hook Bait

Tin Mill Dam

Soughley Lane, Wortley, Deepcar, Sheffield.

Description: This dam is in two halves. The first part you come to is the Carp Pond which contains mainly carp, some over 20lbs. The average fish caught is over 6lbs. Also present are roach, bream, chub, gudgeon and perch. The far dam is what they call the 'silver fish side' and contains roach, bream, small carp, crucian carp, tench, perch, chub and other species.

The river is ideal for fly fishing in some stretches and for coarse fishing in other areas, it contains barbel, chub, dace, trout, grayling, perch and roach. The club has spent some £10,000 plus on the stocking of the river in the past. The stretch of river runs from Deepcar to the back of Bramalls Ponds (Near Thurgoland).

Directions: Come off the A616 Stocksbridge bypass at Deepcar and turn onto Wortley road. Turn left where it meets Soughley Lane and follow the track to the dam.

Ticket Price: Full Members £35, ladies, oap's, disabled £20, juniors £15.

Species: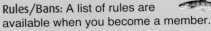

Rules/Bans: A list of rules are available when you become a member.

Facilities:

Best Bait: Luncheon meat or pellet.

47
Fishery Location
See page 6

Number of Lakes: Two, plus a stretch of river.

Nearest Tackle Shop: Kerfoot's Fishing Tackle (see page 78)

Telephone: Phone between 10am to 8pm on 0114 2883728

Best Catch	Peg No:	Weather:		Time of Day:	Date:
Species	Weight	Method (Line & Hook Size)		Ground Bait	Hook Bait

Tinkers Pond

Woodstock Road, Barnsley.

SAT NAV S75 1DX

Description: There are two ponds at tinkers, the top pond which is mainly stocked with carp up to double figures. There's also good head of tench and plenty of roach, rudd, perch and the odd bream. The pond has a depth of up to 14ft in the middle and has 20 pegs. The bottom pond is mainly stocked with skimmers and the odd good bream, roach, rudd and a few chub. You can drive to your peg on half of the pond but be early in the summer months. The venue is good for disabled users as the near side pegs are wheelchair friendly with parking close by.

Directions: From Barnsley city centre head towards Huddersfield on the A635. When you pass Barnsley College turn right on to Woodstock Road. Follow the road to the end, go under the railway bridge, and you will find the ponds on your right.

Ticket Price: Day tickets £4.00. Under 16s and over 65s £2.00. Year ticket £30.00. Concession £15.00.

Species:

Facilities:

Rules/Bans: No bait bans only nuts. No braided hooklengths. No double hooking. No floating baits. No tin cans allowed on the bank. No carp in keepnets - except in matches.

Best Bait: Tench like worm and corn fished quietly in the margins.

Number of Lakes: Two

Number of Pegs: Around 30

48
Fishery Location
See page 6

Nearest Tackle Shop: Barnsley Bait Company (Details page 78)
Telephone: 01226 203090

Best Catch	Peg No:	Weather:		Time of Day:	Date:
Species	Weight	Method (Line & Hook Size)		Ground Bait	Hook Bait

Torne Bank Fishery

West End Road, Located just outside the village of Epworth.

Top Tip
The fish seem to move with the wind and the corner pegs are most popular for that reason.

Description: This is a very well run little fishery which is ideal for a few days away where you can stay on their caravan and camp site. The pond has only 25 pegs with a large island in the middle however fishing is unfortunately not allowed from the island. Fishing the margins with a 6mm soft hookable pellet over a bed of feed pellets which have to be bought on site worked really well for the hungry carp. Many pole anglers were targeting the same fish tight up to the island. If all fails resort to a red maggot up in the water for the numerous roach.

Directions: From the M180, Junction 2 head for Belton. Turn right at the roundabout and follow the road to Sandtoft. When you reach the roundabout in Sandtoft take the first left and continue for nearly a mile. The fishery is signposted on your right.

Ticket Price: Day tickets £5.00 Mon-Fri £6.00 at the weekend.

Species:

Rules/Bans: Barbless only (max, size 12) No method feeder (fixed) No floating baits. No cat/dog meat. All dogs to be on lead. No braided lines. All nets must be seen to be air dried prior to use. (Keepnets only to be used in matches)

Facilities: Accommodates five caravans, with electrical hookups.

       Best Bait: Pellet.

Number of Pegs: 25   **Number of Lakes:** One

Nearest Tackle Shop: Good selection of baits are available on site.

Telephone: 07776 096181

Best Catch	Peg No:	Weather:		Time of Day:	Date:
Species	Weight	Method (Line & Hook Size)		Ground Bait	Hook Bait

Triangs Fishery

Tythe Farm, Kirton Lane, Thorne.

 SAT DN8 5RJ NAV

Description: Four excellent waters here. Kingfisher is for year book holders only, but there is plenty of room on the other lakes. Heron pool with 20 pegs is stuffed with a variety of species but the tench do seem to be the dominant fish. At Willow pond depths vary from 5 feet to 10 feet and has been stocked mainly with carp. There is a small island which when fished close to gives the best results. Great tench fishing and some large carp to have a go at. Superb place to take kids to teach them how to fish.

Directions: From the M180 Junction 1, take the A614 towards Thorne. Turn left just before the canal flyover and head towards Stainforth. Turn right just after crossing the railway lines into Kirton Lane. You need to open the gates to cross back over the railway line (ring from phone at side of track first). The fishery is a few hundred yards on your left.

Ticket Price: Day Ticket £6.00. 7am to an hour before dusk.

Species:

Rules/Bans: No ground bait, boilies, nuts, cat or dog food. No night fishing. Under 14s must be accompanied by an adult. No keepnets, barbless hooks only.

Facilities: **Number of Lakes:** Four
Number of Pegs: Over 100

Best Bait: Pellet and paste.

Nearest Tackle Shop: First for Fishing (Details page 78)

Telephone: 01405 816402 or 07890 167407

50
Fishery location
See page 6

Best Catch	Peg No:	Weather:		Time of Day:	Date:
Species	Weight	Method (Line & Hook Size)		Ground Bait	Hook Bait

Tyram Hall Fishery

Moor Dike Road, Hatfield Woodhouse, Doncaster.

SAT NAV DN7 6DR

Description: The Island Lake is the first lake you come to on the complex, which holds a very large head of carp from 3 to 20lb. There are approx. 40 pegs, with an island running straight down the middle. There are many features with over hanging trees, planted reeds and pads. From pegs 1 to 20 you are looking at depths from 3 to 12ft, whilst pegs 21 to 40 are more platform with depths from 2 to 8ft. The lake it self is a great all rounder for most anglers. With method feeder tight to the island, pellet waggler half way across and don't forget the margins. The Carp Lake has some very big fish around the 30lb mark. There are also some large pike at this fishery - weights up to 25lb have been landed in the past.

Directions: Heading South on the A18, take the A614 to Bawtry. Go through Hatfield Woodhouse and take a left to the carpark.

Ticket Price: Day tickets Coarse Lake £5.00. OAP's & Under 14's £5.00. Carp Lake £10.00 upto 3 rods. 24hr £15.00

Species:

Facilities:

Rules/Bans: No keepnets, barbless hooks only. See other rules on-site.

Best Bait: Mussels, paste or pellet.

Number of Pegs: Around 90

Number of Lakes: Four

Nearest Tackle Shop: Stainforth Angling Centre.

Telephone: 01302 840886

51 Fishery Location See page 6

Top Tip

Try fishing down the edge using mussels or paste!

Best Catch	Peg No:	Weather:		Time of Day:	Date:
Species	Weight	Method (Line & Hook Size)		Ground Bait	Hook Bait

Westwood Reservoir

Downland Avenue, High Green, Sheffield.

Description: This is an excellent all year round venue. Great for roach in the colder months. Like a lot of reservoirs this one is very deep and can reach over 19 feet in places. A great water to fish with plenty of species to target, however it has only got 40 pegs and can get busy especially on match days. A few pegs near to the car park are suitable for the disabled angler as further along the bank it becomes fairly steep.

Directions: From the M1 Junction 36, head towards Sheffield on the A61. When you reach High Green turn left onto Wortley Road. After a short distance turn left into Westwood Road. Turn next right into Downland Avenue and follow this road to the bottom where you will find the reservoir.

Top Tip

Waggler fishing can be effective but a slow sink will provide the best results

Ticket Price: Day Tickets £4.00. Year permits £30.00 starting in March. Concession £20.00. Juvenile £10.00.

Species:

Facilities:

Rules/Bans: No keepnets, barbless hooks only. No bloodworm or joker.

Best Bait: The carp will fall to specimen tactics with boilies, meat or corn. Red worm for the tench.

Number of Pegs: 40

Number of Lakes: One

Nearest Tackle Shop: D J Angling (Details on page 78)

Telephone: 0779 9447145

52

Best Catch	Peg No:	Weather:		Time of Day:	Date:
Species	Weight	Method (Line & Hook Size)		Ground Bait	Hook Bait

West End Fisheries

Boiley Lane, Killamarsh, Sheffield.

Top Tip
Try pole fishing as close to the corner of the islands for the larger carp

Description: This fishery has been well stocked with carp, roach, rudd, bream and tench. The main lake has 50 pegs some situated in an island in the middle of the lake. Targeting these small islands gives you the best chance of catching the numerous carp present. A recently new lake with 22 pegs has been built for both pleasure and match fishing. Carp, rudd, bream, tench, and roach can be found in good numbers in all lakes.

Directions: At the main shopping area in Killamarsh turn up Bridge St, and turn right at the Nags Head public house. Keep going on this road until you get to the West End pub where you turn right, then immediately left onto Boiley Lane. Follow the track to an old railway bridge, turn right into the car park.

Ticket Price: £6.00 per day. OAPs £4.00 Mon-Fri.
Year permits £65.00 which includes KJS and Aston Springs fisheries (13 ponds in total).

Species: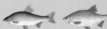

Rules/Bans: Barbless hooks only. No keepnets. All anglers must use a landing net. No ground bait except in a cup or feeder. Under 16's must be accompanied by an adult.

Facilities:
Cafe open in summer months.

Best Bait: Meat, corn, maggot and caster.

Number of Lakes: Three

Nearest Tackle Shop: Bankside Tackle (Details on page 78)

Telephone: 0114 2470876

53
Fishery Location
See page 6

Best Catch	Peg No:	Weather:		Time of Day:	Date:
Species	Weight	Method (Line & Hook Size)		Ground Bait	Hook Bait

Willow Garth Ponds

Shaftholme Road, Arksey, Doncaster.

Top Tip

Try hair-rigged luncheon meat for the large carp and tench

Description: There are two well established lakes on the fishery offering a total of 40 to 45 pegs both containing good stocks of quality roach that have been caught to over 2lb, as well as huge quantities of small roach and rudd, perch, tench a few bream and golden orfe. The fishery is also renowned for its big carp with fish close to thirty pounds having been recorded. Work on digging out a third lake for commercial type carping has been planned for sometime in the future. Silver fish in abundance but be careful of the pike, ranging from 2-15lb as they like to ambush hooked fish.

Directions: Head towards Bentley on the A19. Turn right when you see the sign post for Arksey. Follow this road until you see a turn on to Shaftholme Lane. Cross over the railway line into Shaftholme Road. You will see the fishery on your right.

Ticket Price: Day tickets are £4.00. Juniors £3.00. Evenings £3.00 / £2.00. Night fishing £8.00.

Species:

Facilities:

Rules/Bans: No keepnets, barbless hooks only.

Best Bait: Maggot, meat or pellet.

Number of Pegs: Around 45

Number of Lakes: Two

54

Fishery Location
See page 6

Nearest Tackle Shop: Kingfisher Angling Centre (see page 78)

Telephone: 01302 563728

Best Catch	Peg No:	Weather:		Time of Day:	Date:
Species	Weight	Method (Line & Hook Size)		Ground Bait	Hook Bait

60

Wire Mill Dam Fishery

Whiteley Wood Road, Sheffield.

SAT NAV: S11 7FF

Top Tip
Fish close to the lillies as you dare, thats where the carp and tench hold up

Description: Great for beginners with plenty of roach, perch, tench, and a good head of crucian carp. It is quite shallow at only 4 feet at its deepest but this dam is full of fish and during the summer months maggot or sweet corn will catch all day long. Try feeder fishing to the far bank where many of the larger fish hold up. Use luncheon meat hair rigged for the numerous tench that reach 6lb. This tactic also works for the carp which reach 17lbs. The high quality roach and perch also makes this water one of the best winter fishing venues in the area. Recently re-stocked with mirror and common carp.

Directions: From Sheffield take the A625 (Ecclesall Road). Turn right on to Knowle Lane after passing the Prince of Wales Pub. Continue up Knowle Lane and turn right 600 metres past the Hammer and Pincers Pub. Follow the road for about 1 mile and you will find the dam and car park on your left.

Ticket Price: Day Tickets £4.00. Year Permits £40.00 Concession year permits £30.00

Species:

Rules/Bans: Barbless hooks only, no keepnets except in matches, no night fishing. Ground bait in pole cup or feeder only. No floating baits.

Facilities:

Number of Pegs: Around 20
Number of Lakes: One

Fishery Location
See page 6

Best Bait: Maggot or bread punch for the silver fish. Soft hookable pellets for the crucian carp. Luncheon meat or sweetcorn for the tench and carp

Nearest Tackle Shop: Billy Clarke Tackle Shop (see page 65)

Telephone: 07809 172872

Best Catch	Peg No:	Weather:		Time of Day:	Date:
Species	Weight	Method (Line & Hook Size)		Ground Bait	Hook Bait

Wombwell Dam

SAT NAV: S74 9SZ

Woodhead Lane, Wombwell, Barnsley.

Top Tip
The double-figure fish in the larger pool tend to be found in the deeper water towards the dam end.

Description: This peaceful fishery consists of two ponds situated inside Wombwell Woods near Barnsley. The smaller top pond contains a lower quantity of big fish but it is a great place for bream, roach and carp. The bigger bottom pond contains bigger fish with specimen carp over 25lb along with tonnes of skimmers and roach. Feeder, pole and waggler all catch well on this venue. The pegs in the narrower area away from the dam wall seem to be the hotspots.

Directions: From Junction 36 of the M1, take the A6095 signposted Wombwell. After about 3 miles, at the fifth roundabout turn left onto Woodhead Lane. After a hundred yards turn right onto a dirt track and follow this down to the carpark. The waters are a short walk through the trees.

Ticket Price: Day tickets £5.00 (Bottom Lake) £4.00 (Top Lake) £3.00 for children. £1.00 cheaper on each pond after 4pm.

Species:

Facilities: P

Rules/Bans: Barbless hooks only, no bread, no floating baits. No cat or dog meat. No night fishing.

Best Bait: Chopped worm or double red maggot.

Number of Pegs: N/A

Number of Lakes: Two

56
Fishery Location
See page 6

Nearest Tackle Shop: Fishing Republic (Details on page 78)

Telephone: 07932 333276

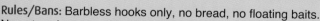

Best Catch	Peg No:	Weather:		Time of Day:	Date:
Species	Weight	Method (Line & Hook Size)		Ground Bait	Hook Bait

Woodhouse Grange

Bawtry Road, Hatfield Woodhouse, Doncaster.

Top Tip
Swap between two margin swims, feeding micro pellets to keep a stream of fish coming

Description: There are six waters to choose from. Heron, Cobbie and Kingfisher lakes house the heavier carp to 30lbs. Ghost Lake has plenty of silver fish with carp to 12lb and Kennel Lake which is the largest with 37 pegs has tench to 9lb. These are excellent ponds with plenty of quality fish to target. Everyone seemed to be catching on the day I went, fishing at a poles length with a single white maggot worked for me. Ghost Lake has margin reeds either side of most pegs so I fished each side with my top 2 plus 1 section with great success. Also try feeder fishing large pellets or corn during the summer months for the larger fish.

Directions: From Bawtry head north on the A614. Go through Blaxton and you will find the fishery on your right just before you reach Hatfield Woodhouse.

Ticket Price: Day tickets £6.00 from the cafe.

Species:

Rules/Bans: No bloodworm or joker, no hemp seed or tares, no boilies or nuts, no method feeder. Barbless 12 max hooks. No keepnets. Ground baits in small feeder or pole cup.

Facilities: Bait can be bought from the shop within the cafe.

Number of Pegs: 226   **Number of Lakes:** Six

Best Bait: Micro's for feed and 6mm expander pellets for the hook. Maggot and corn both work well.

Fishery Location See page 6 — 57

Nearest Tackle Shop: Stainforth Angling Centre (Details page 78)

Telephone: Call bailiff: Mark on 07936 647588

Best Catch	Peg No:	Weather:		Time of Day:	Date:
Species	Weight	Method (Line & Hook Size)		Ground Bait	Hook Bait

Worsbrough Reservoir

A61, Sheffield Road, Barnsley.

Description: There are 80 pegs to fish at Worsbrough with trees to one side and stone banks to the other. The depths vary from the shallows to around 15 feet at the dam head. This reservoir is fished by top match anglers all year round. There are a lot of bream to the 5lb mark with roach to 2lb and many big perch. You can also find pike with many reaching 14lbs and some good quality tench. The reservoir has recently been re-stocked with 4000 carp.

Directions: Coming from Barnsley take the A61 south. When you get to Worsbrough go through a set of traffic lights and turn right into Worsbrough Mill Country Park, across the road from the Button Mill pub.

Ticket Price: Day tickets £4.00. Under 16s and over 65s £2.00. Year ticket £30.00. Concession £15.00.

Species:

Facilities:

Rules/Bans: No bait bans only nuts. No braided hooklengths. No double hooking. No floating baits. No tin cans allowed on the bank. No carp in keepnets - except in matches.

Best Bait: Worm or caster.

Number of Pegs: 80

Number of Lakes: One

Nearest Tackle Shop: Barnsley Angling. (see page 78)

Telephone: 01226 203090

Fishery Location
See page 6

Best Catch	Peg No:	Weather:		Time of Day:	Date:
Species	Weight	Method (Line & Hook Size)		Ground Bait	Hook Bait

Fishery Index

Pole Fishing

FOR THE BEGINNER

Of all the different methods of fishing I've tried, I haven't found any of them as accurate or as easy as pole fishing. To be able to place your bait and feed to the exact spot, sometimes only inches from an island or group of reeds is what makes pole fishing so productive and fun.

TACKLE NEEDED

A Pole

Poles come in various sizes, from 4 metres (usually called a whip) to poles of 18.5 metres. They also vary dramatically in price as well which is usually governed by weight and rigidity. The lighter and straighter (no droop at the end) the more expensive they are. I recommend a pole between 11 and 13 metres, stay away from the smaller telescopic ones. Many tackle shops have poles ready assembled for you to handle, make sure you are comfortable with its weight and it feels well balanced. Test that it takes apart smoothly. If possible, get a pole with a spare top section as they enable you to rig up for different species and size of fish.

Pole Rigs

Experienced anglers can make up their own pole rigs but beginners are advised to buy ready-made. There are plenty of quality ready made rigs available for as little as £2.99. These rigs come with a main line with a loop on the end (used to attach the line to the stonfo connector at the tip of your pole). A float with enough shot below it to cock it nicely in the water and a length of lower breaking strain line which has a spade end hook tied to it. The float and shot can slide down the line and be adjusted accordingly.

Pole Elastic

The elastic that runs through the top sections of your pole cushions the fight of a hooked fish and allows you to play it. Elastics are graded in sizes 1-20.
The following list is a good guide for the beginner:
1. For small roach and perch for example - use a No4 elastic with a 1lb hook length and a 2lb main line.
2. If fishing for small carp and tench or skimmer bream use a No8 or 10 elastic with a 3.5lb main line and 2.5lb hook length.
3. When fishing for carp up to 12lbs use a No16 to 18 elastic, and a main line of 8lb with a 6.5lb hook length.

START TO FISH

Fishing Position

Get your seatbox in position. Ideally, when sitting on the box your thighs should be in a horizontal position at right angles to your lower leg. Holding the pole correctly makes it comfortable for long periods and prevents backache. For a right handed person you need to rest the pole across your knees with your left hand supporting it. Put your right forearm along the end of the pole and firmly grip the pole with your right hand. Have close to hand - your bait, landing net, disgorger and anything else you may require for your days fishing. It is important to have your pole roller in the correct location. The pole has to be well balanced in your hands when it leaves the roller - this prevents rig tangles when shipping out.

Start Fishing

You have set up your pole and plumbed your depth - so now you are ready to fish. Make sure you have between 10" and 20" of line between the tip and float. In more windy conditions you may want to lengthen this. Feed your swim with groundbait (if allowed) plus a few bits of your hook bait. This is more accurately done using a pole cup which can be fixed to the end of your pole. Put your bait on the hook and ship out your pole trying to keep your rig in the water as this prevents tangles. Lay the rig on the water lengthways. The shot on the line will pull the line under the water and cock the float. Enjoy your first pole fishing day!

South Yorkshire Rivers

River Dearne
Denaby Main

Description: This stretch of the River Dearne is run by the Denaby Miners Welfare Angling Club and comprises of 60 pegs from the Pastures Road Bridge to the confluence with the River Don at Denaby Main. Twenty species of fish have been recorded in the last few years. The dominant fish have been skimmers, hybrid's, roach, chub, perch, gudgeon, and dace. Chub to 3lb are a regular size catch. The highest pleasure fishing weight record is 49lbs 15oz consisting of 184 roach and a single skimmer caught with a waggler and caster.

Directions: From the A1 follow the signs for the Denaby Main, carry on through Denaby Main up to the roundabout, go right at the roundabout over the River Don and canal and turn right at the ATS garage onto Pastures Road. Carry on down the road past the Pasture Lodge Motel, go over the River Dearne bridge then turn immediately right into the car park. Finally go over the stile and you are on the banks of the River Dearne.

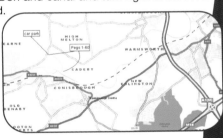

Ticket Price: Day tickets and season permits are available.

Species:

Best Bait: Maggot or caster.

Nearest Tackle Shop: Paul's Tackle Centre (see page 78)

Telephone: 01709 864037

Information kindly supplied by the Denaby Miners Welfare A.C.

Best Catch	Peg No:	Weather:		Time of Day:	Date:
Species	Weight	Method (Line & Hook Size)	Ground Bait		Hook Bait

River Don

Doncaster, Hexthorpe and Sprotborough.

Description: Doncaster & D.A.A. control the fishing rights on the Don from Sprotborough Weir and downstream to Crimpsall Sluice near Doncaster Prison. The river is deep, up to 15 feet down the centre, with a width of around 30 metres. Because of the depth, fish can be caught all year round. In fact it's not uncommon for big bags on some of the colder winter days. At usual level the river is slow, almost still at times, but be careful when it's been raining. Because the banks are steep the river is prone to rising quickly. Even a foot of extra water will make the river very difficult to fish.

The main species to be caught are roach, skimmers, perch, barbel and chub, but dace, bream, pike, eels and even carp can be found. The barbel average around 3 to 5 lbs but bigger fish have been caught and they're getting bigger every year. Bags of small fish can top 20lbs on a good day, but 10lbs is still a good catch.

Methods:

One of the great things about the River Don is that fish can be caught on the pole, stick float, waggler, topper, slider, ground bait feeder, bomb and almost any method you can think of.

For the barbel try meat or pellet on the hook over a bed of hemp. If you can find a patch of gravel the barbel will find you.

For the chub, look for pegs with overhanging trees or a crease in the current. The classic combination of hemp and caster should do the trick.

For the roach and skimmer you can loose feed, but the depth means that it is usually better to fish over a bed of groundbait. The pole is the obvious choice when the river is at normal level, but a float on running line is better when the river is up 6 inches or so. Try pinkies, maggots or caster.

Sprotborough Weir

River Don, Hexthorpe

Eden Grove, Hexthorpe

Rigs:

If you're after the barbel or chub they can be had on the usual feeder or bomb setups, but don't discount the stick float or waggler. Try running a heavy float with plenty of shot down the line. You can drag up to a couple of feet along the bottom to slow the bait down as most pegs are snag free with a sandy bottom. Hooklengths should be around at least 3 to 4lb. Hooks should suit your bait size, but a size 14 will give you plenty of leverage should you hook a big 'un. The roach and skimmers can be a little cute, so you'll have to scale your rigs down, whether you use the pole or running line. Hooklengths as light as 1lb (0.006) are sometimes the only way you can get bites.

Directions:

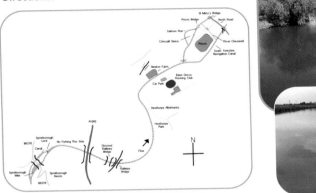

Ticket Price: Day ticket £4.00. Books are valid from April 1st at £22.00. Concessionary rates £17.00 available for OAP's and Juniors.

Species:

Rules/Bans:

No fires or camping allowed. No night fishing. No live baits. No cars or motorcycles allowed on banks. No wasp grub. Bloodworm and joker is only allowed between Oct and March. No litter to be left on banks. Keep to recognised footpath. Close all gates.

Best Bait: Maggot or caster.

Nearest Tackle Shop: Paul's Tackle Centre (Details on page 78)

Telephone: 07771 986849

Information kindly supplied by Doncaster & District Angling Association.

Best Catch	Peg No:	Weather:		Time of Day:	Date:
Species	Weight	Method (Line & Hook Size)	Ground Bait		Hook Bait

River Idle

Bawtry, Newington, Mission.

Description: The river in most places is between 12 and 20 feet wide, with depths from 4 to 7 feet. The water runs at an easy pace and I found using a stick float with a single red maggot worked well but to avoid the gudgeon try a bit of corn. There's a very good stock of silver fish with roach over two pounds. Good size bream have been caught - some to six pounds. Chub and perch make up the other dominant species. This river is also great for piking with some old ones reaching twenty pounds.

Directions: Bawtry: Leave the A1 and take the A631 (Bawtry Rd) signposted Bawtry. Proceed through High Street and turn left onto Wharf Street. Park and take the footpath under the viaduct and follow this path to the left which will take you to the river.

Newington: From Bawtry take the A164 heading to Finningley. When you reach Newington turn right at the Ship Inn and park.

Mission: From Newington take the Bawtry Road and after a mile or so you will reach Mission. Drive through the village and turn right into River Lane. Follow the lane to the river.

Ticket Price: Day tickets available on the bank.

Species:

Best Bait: Worm, maggot or caster.

Nearest Tackle Shop: R&R Sports (Details on page 78)

Fishery location
See page 68
3

Best Catch	Peg No:	Weather:		Time of Day:	Date:
Species	Weight	Method (Line & Hook Size)		Ground Bait	Hook Bait

River Rother Catcliffe, Sheffield.

Description: Who would have thought that the once 'most polluted river' in the country would have turned out to be a vastly improving fishery? We are talking about the Rother in Catcliffe.

Catcliffe, Brinsworth and Treeton Anglers Alliance have control of a mile of river at Catcliffe and believe me it produces some very good fish. Big perch! The best up to now being a 4 pounder taken by Mick Kitchin in a match when he had eight perch for 21 pounds. There are also some very good chub up to 5lbs with a few 2 pound roach. Some very good barbel, carp and pike, dace and gudgeon, also trout up to 4 pounds. There are 50 platforms, 23 of these are 4 foot wide and 5 foot long - these are ideal for the disabled angler. The fishery offers many good aspects of fishing. Its diversity offers good sport to the many different types of fishing with some very deep slow glides to faster shallow swims, making it ideal for float or ledger fishing, or spinning for pike, perch and trout.

Philip Baker with a 13lb 4oz barbel caught in the River Rother at Catcliffe, Sheffield

Directions: It is easy to find by car just off the M1 motorway, Junction 33, via the Sheffield Parkway to the village of Catcliffe. The river runs alongside Orgreave Road with free parking at both ends of the fishery via The Plough public house.

Ticket Price: Day ticket £3.00. Concessions £1.50.
Adult season tickets £12.00. OAP's and children under 16 £6.00.
Children under 12 can fish for free if accompanied by an adult who is also fishing.

Species:

Best Bait: Maggot, caster and meat for the barbel.

Nearest Tackle Shop: Fishing Republic. (see page 78)

Telephone: 07774 884946

Facilities:

Information kindly supplied by Clive Nuttall Secretary of Catcliffe, Brinsworth, Treeton Anglers Alliance.

Best Catch	Peg No:	Weather:		Time of Day:	Date:
Species	Weight	Method (Line & Hook Size)		Ground Bait	Hook Bait

River Torne

Epworth Road Bridge to Pilfrey Bridge.

Description: Technically this section is in North Lincolnshire. The river is more of a drain than a river and is close to the border with South Yorkshire. It's only around 13 metres wide but there is a little variety where sections of rushes extend into the water. Depth is around 4 or 5 feet. In summer the river can be slow, weedy and clear, but in winter the water is usually coloured due to water being pumped off the fields. Roach are the predominant species, but the river is probably most famous for its pike population. Plenty of fish to over 20lbs are caught every year and jacks to mid singles are commonplace.

Methods: For the pike deadbaits are king, but spinning comes a very close second. Caster, punched bread or pinkie are the key baits for the roach. Hemp and tares can be great if you find big shoal of roach. Pole fishing with a long line is often best but be careful of spooking the fish in the clear water. Small amounts of loose feed should be fed regularly. If bites don't come quickly try feeding and fishing further downstream to draw the fish up, then bring them up the river by feeding back at your starting point.

Rigs: Fish light rigs with No.11 shot or even better, No.9 leads spread out so that the bait falls naturally through the water at the same speed as your loose feed. Many of your bites from the roach will come on the drop and will be sharp, so be alert. Experiment with different feeding patterns until the bites become easier to hit. Don't go too light with the lines because of the weed. Try around 1.5 to 2lbs with hooks around a size 22.

Directions: Epworth Road Bridge to Pilfrey Bridge on the A18 - a stretch of about 15 miles. Access may be gained at various road bridges.

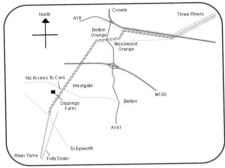

The River Torne
Epworth Bridge to
Belton Bridge
Please refer to the map. There is no vehicular access from Belton Bridge upstream past Dippings Farm towards Epworth Road Bridge. Anglers must park at Belton Bridge and walk upstream. Alternatively, anglers may drive downstream from Epworth Bridge but not past Dippings Farm. Anglers using this water must park off the track to allow the safe passage of farm vehicles and lorries. This track is private property. Please respect the owners' wishes and the agreements that the Association has made with the owners.

The River Torne at Belton Grange.

The River Torne near Mosswood Grange

Ticket Price: Day ticket £4.00. Books are valid from April 1st at £22.00. Concessionary rates £17.00 available for OAP's and Juniors.

Species:

Rules/Bans:
No fires or camping allowed. No night fishing. No live baits. No cars or motorcycles allowed on banks. No wasp grub. Bloodworm and joker is only allowed between Oct and March. No litter to be left on banks. Keep to recognised footpath. Close all gates.

Best Bait: Maggot or caster.

Nearest Tackle Shop: Barries Fishing Tackle (see page 78)

Telephone: 07771 986849

5
Fishery Location
See page 68

Information kindly supplied by Doncaster & District Angling Association.

Best Catch	Peg No:	Weather:		Time of Day:	Date:	
Species	Weight	Method (Line & Hook Size)		Ground Bait	Hook Bait	75

LOG-IT (keep a note of your best catch)

Venue:							Date:
Peg No:	Start Time:	End Time:	Weather Conditions:				

Species	Weight	Method	Rig set up	Ground Bait	Hook Bait	Time

LOG–IT (keep a note of your best catch)

Venue:

Date:

Peg No:

Start Time:

End Time:

Weather Conditions:

Species	Weight	Method	Rig set up	Ground Bait	Hook Bait	Time

South Yorkshire Tackle Shops

Alan's Fishing Tackle, 111 Main St, Bramley, Rotherham, S66 2SE. 01709 702454

Bag-Up Angling Supplies, 37 Station Rd, Chapeltown, S35 2XH 0114 2466670

Bankside Tackle, Enterprise Way, Holbrook, Sheffield S20 3GL 0114 2488177

Barnsley Angling, 48-50 Sheffield Rd, Birdwell, Barnsley. S74 0DQ 07570 122726

Barnsley Bait Company, 85a Towngate, Barnsley S75 6AS 01226 210183

Barries Fishing Tackle, 14 King Avenue, Doncaster. DN11 0PG. 01302 863832

Billy Clarke, 77-81 Alderson Rd, Sheffield, S2 4UB. 0114 2551145

Climax Fishing Tackle Ltd, 2 Stubley Hollow, Dronfield. S18 1PP 01246 291155

Cookes Angling Supplies, 3 Greasborough Rd, Rotherham. 01709 820579

Dawson's Of Hillsborough, 70-72 Holme Lane, Sheffield, S6 4JW. 0114 2812178

Decathlon, Eyre St, Sheffield, S1 4QZ. 0114 2298190

DJ Angling, 104 Greengate Lane, High Green, S35 3GT 0114 2847576

Doncaster Angling Centre, 207 Carr House Rd, Doncaster. 01302 363629

D & P Fishing Tackle, 38 Laughton Rd. Dinnington, S25 2PS 01909 519456

First For Fishing, Frontier Works, King Edward Road, Thorne DN8 4HU 01405 818277

Fishing Republic, Snape Hill Rd, Darfield, Barnsley, S73 9JU. 01226 752300

Fishing Republic, 12 Stoke Street, Attercliffe, Sheffield. S9 3QD 0114 2441339

Kingfisher Angling Centre, 148 High St, Bentley, Doncaster, DN5 0AT. 01302 874888

Ian's Fishing Tackle Shop, 303 Prince Of Wales Rd, Sheffield. 0114 2531533

Kerfoot's Fishing Tackle, 6 Southey Green Rd, Sheffield, S5 8GW. 0114 2313265

Mosborough Tackle Box, 38b High St, Sheffield, S19 5AE. 0114 2510664

Parkgate Angling Centre, 19 Broad St, Parkgate, Rotherham, S62 6DX. 01709 527297

Pauls Fishing Tackle Centre, Doncaster Rd, Doncaster DN12 4HU. 01709 862558

R & R Sports, 40 High St, Bawtry, Doncaster, DN10 6JE. 01302 711130

Six A.M Tackle + Bait, 82 Worksop Rd, Swallownest, Sheffield. 0114 2873070

Stainforth Angling Ctr, 24 Silver St, Stainforth, Doncaster DN7 5AH. 01302 846623

Supabait, Clifton Lane, Clifton, Doncaster, DN12 2AL. 01709 863341

Tackle 2 Fish, Unit 2-5 Penistone Rd Trading Estate, Sheffield, S6 2FL 0114 2323696

Tardis Tackle Angling Centre, 346 Sheffield Road, Barnsley. 01226 350838

Tardis Tackle Angling Centre, 4 Sicey Ave, Sheffield. 0114 2436655

Tealys Tackle Shop, 53 High Street, Goldthorpe, Rotherham, S63 9LQ 01709 880679

Thorne Pet & Angling, 5 The Green, Thorne, Doncaster, DN8 5AP. 01405 814056

Intake Angling Supplies, 27a Mansfield Rd, Sheffield S12 2AE. 0114 2649664

Wickersley Angling Centre, 2-4 Hellaby Ind Est, Rotherham, S66 8HR 01709 540998

Woodseats Angling, 625 Chesterfield Rd, Sheffield S8 0RX. 0114 2585133